The
Latchkey Dog

The Latchkey Dog

How the Way You Live Shapes the Behavior

of the Dog You Love

Jodi Andersen

Quill

A HarperResource Book

An Imprint of HarperCollinsPublishers

*Author's Note: The names and details
of the training examples in this book have
been changed when necessary to respect
the confidentiality of the working relationships*

A hardcover edition of this book was published by HarperCollins Publishers in 2000.

THE LATCHKEY DOG. Copyright © 2000 by Jodi Andersen. Photographs copyright © 2000 by Dennis Mosner. All rights reserved. Printed in the United States of America. No part of this book may be used or reproduced in any manner whatsoever without written permission except in the case of brief quotations embodied in critical articles and reviews. For information address HarperCollins Publishers Inc., 10 East 53rd Street, New York, NY 10022.

HarperCollins books may be purchased for educational, business, or sales promotional use. For information please write: Special Markets Department, HarperCollins Publishers Inc., 10 East 53rd Street, New York, NY 10022.

First HarperResource Quill paperback edition published 2002

Designed by Judith Stagnitto Abbate

The Library of Congress has catalogued the hardcover edition as follows:
Andersen, Jodi, 1958–
The latchkey dog: how the way you live shapes the behavior of the dog you love/ by Jodi Andersen.—1st ed.
p. cm.
ISBN 0-06-270240-8
1. Dogs–Behavior.   I.Title

SF433.A52 2000
636.7'0887–dc21

                                                00-39625

ISBN 0-06-273666-3 (pbk.)

02 03 04 05 06 RRD 10 9 8 7 6 5 4 3 2 1

For Alexandra and Olivia,
who inspire me to dream

Contents

Acknowledgments

No completed book, regardless of its author, is ever the result of a single effort. It is a collaborative work credited not only to the writer but to that writer's support system of family, friends, and colleagues. In other words, "it takes a village." *The Latchkey Dog* is no exception, and it is with immeasurable gratitude that I express thanks to those who made up my village.

To begin, I am profoundly grateful to my agent and friend, Joni Evans, for believing that my work with dogs was worth sharing on a grander scale. Her encouragement and guidance have opened doors that a novice writer only dreams of walking through. I am forever in her debt. A thousand thanks to Phyllis Levy, whose love of all creatures has led her and so many wonderful people into my life. She has undoubtedly had a hand in the course of my destiny and I am eternally grateful. My gratitude as well to Trish Medved, whose initial interest in the book's outline gave it life.

To my wonderful editor, Robert Jones, whose expertise not only as an editor and writer but also as a dog lover helped to shape *The Latchkey Dog* into an accessible, finished work that I am truly proud of. So many thanks to Fiona Hallowell and Jennifer Sherwood for providing me with information and guidance that saved me from many an embarrassing moment.

Many thanks as well to Drs. Paul Schwartz and Gene Solomon, along with the entire staff at The Center for Veterinary Care, for their continued and unbending support of my work.

A huge thank-you to Dennis Mosner for his fabulous photographic contribution to *The Latchkey Dog*, and to Elise Caputo whose selfless efforts to champion this book have gone far above and beyond the call of duty.

To all of my clients, many of whom I am privileged to say have become friends—thank you for allowing me to share in countless personal moments that have given me valuable insight into how our relationships with our dogs can profoundly affect their behavior. I cannot mention them all by name but standing tall among them are Joan Gelman, Amanda Mecke, and Mary Ann Zeeman. Their advice and encouragement helped me to take the first step as a writer and sustained me throughout the entire process.

To my family and friends, I give extra thanks. To my sisters, Anne Marie Sorkin and Randi Levine, who have always made me feel that I could accomplish anything I set out to do and then helped me do it. To my parents, Sandy and Chuck Fiesel, who allowed me to drag home just about every homeless animal I could find. And to my father, Stuart Lesser, who took me to pet shop after pet shop, Sunday after Sunday, just to "look" at the puppies.

To my dear friend Patty Caruso, whose belief in my talent and in this book might possibly turn *The Latchkey Dog* into a household word. She is a true friend and I could not be more grateful to have her in my corner.

Because thanks can be the swiftest messenger for gratitude, my cup runneth over with thanks to my very best friends, June Mitchell Ingraham and Amy Willen Spiros. Their unbending support, valuable criticism, constant hand-holding, and precise organization of my life turned an otherwise impossible task into a tangible accomplishment. In other words, without them, this book would simply not be a book. From the bottom of my heart, I love them both dearly.

To Alexandra, Olivia, and Jes, the loves of my life, whose immeasurable patience and support over these many months has earned them nothing short of a medal. To my mother-in-law, Hennie Andersen, who is always there, not only as a mother and as a grandmother, but as a friend—I couldn't possibly live without her. To my nephew, Brad Levine, whose constant prodding prompted me to get Blue, the best dog I have ever had the privilege to live with. And finally to Blue, who taught me the most valuable lessons a dog owner needs to know, the most important of which was how to wag a dog.

Introduction

The domesticated dog (*Canis familiaris*) has an ancient lineage believed to go back almost 25,000 years. Negotiating the rules of a complex social structure called a "pack," the dog has survived alongside man when other species could not, and has slowly evolved into the pampered companion of the present day. While this contemporary canine still bears a physical resemblance to his ancient predecessor, sometimes appearance seems to be the only characteristic these two creatures share.

Since roughly the dawn of time, the dog has peacefully coexisted with man, the dog being man's perfect partner. Man and dog had enjoyed a mutual understanding of each other's needs, one that enabled them to share the spoils of the hunt as well as the hunt itself. A relationship developed between the two that was mutually rewarding, and in which the power structure was clearly delineated. The most steadfast of workers, man's canine cohabitant proved time and again that "a good dog was not hard to find."

A consciousness of basic obedience as we know it today never entered the picture. Man simply ruled and dog complied. There was little time in the daily business of survival for puppy kindergarten or private trainers. A meaningful grunt was indeed worth a thousand words. If the hunt was successful, the day's bounty was scraped clean (man, of course, eating first), then man and beast curled up by the fire and dreamed of bigger fish to fry. Companionship was merely a fringe benefit.

This arrangement worked well for centuries but, alas, man saw the opportunity for progress and began to feel cramped. Still, when he left his cave in search of a two-bedroom, one-and-a-half bathroom house, his dog dutifully followed. Never questioning the path of progress, man's best friend was content as long as he remained part of man's pack. But much has changed over the last few thousand years: With leash laws and "No Dogs Allowed" signs at every corner, man has been left with little choice but to "go it alone." The family that once hunted together is now busy scheduling yoga classes, soccer games, and business lunches, leaving the dog "home alone." So much for the good ol' days! In an age of cell phones and cyberspace, it's not just man, but man's canine companion as well, who suffers stress in the face of progress.

Remember the days when you would come home from school and your mother was always there, standing at the front door, with the dog at her side, both happily awaiting your arrival? Then, after a quick snack of milk and cookies, you and your dog spent the remaining daylight hours outside together playing. If your memory bank is coming up empty, it's probably because this is the new millennium and, the chances are, your mother is the CEO of a *Fortune* 500 company (one that perhaps your grandmother founded), milk and cookies have been replaced by rice cakes, and, as far as playing with the dog goes, being on-line is much more fun than being on-leash. With more men and women on career paths that require extended office hours, so that "nine to five" is no longer a part of anybody's job description, the dog, who was for centuries a worker, has now become a waiter.

Whether waiting for his next appointment at the acupuncturist or just waiting around the house, the dog's life no longer revolves around "What can I do?," but instead is focused on "Where is everybody?" Often left to spend the majority of each day organizing their own schedules, these modern mongrels' behavior has become as unpredictable as El Niño. With thousands of years of man/dog relationships under our collars, you'd think by now we would have figured out a healthy way to adapt to cultural changes. Think again. It seems that somewhere between Donna Reed and surfing the Net, what we've ended up with is the latchkey dog.

No longer having to "earn their keep," the latchkey dog is a savvy, upscale, competitive, social (or antisocial, as we will see) canine who can be seen in all the "right places," sporting only the best accessories.

When not out on the town, he is most likely at home listening to the messages on your answering machine, thinking that you just don't spend enough quality time with him anymore. And if his master hasn't filled his day with appointments and activities, he'll just use the time to make toothpicks out of the dining room chairs. Modern man, distracted and busy, hustles so as to satisfy what he thinks his dog needs, but the result is that he might just be ruining the dog altogether.

There is a significant trend emerging in the behavioral problems of dogs who devote their days to waiting. As dog trainers, canine behaviorists, and veterinarians are increasingly called upon to address such sensitive issues as separation anxiety, aggression, and obsessive-compulsive disorders, the time has come to take a closer look at what is really going on. These problems seem to be the result of our current perception of our interaction with our dogs. The man/dog relationship, once built on the foundation of a partnership, has evolved into a dependency, a dependency that swings both ways and which the dog is clearly having a hard time living with.

One might assume that people on career paths requiring extended periods of time away from home each day would recognize that their lifestyles are at odds with a dog's needs. The truth is that more people are choosing a dog as a companion than ever before. No longer is the dog just a family pet. Studies have shown that simply being around animals relieves stress, and dogs are at the top of the list of therapy animals. While dogs providing the modern function of stress relief for us does suggest that the dog is, in fact, doing a job, it is a passive job rather than the active hunting and herding jobs of the past, and, inasmuch as stroking the dog lessens the stress of our daily woes, active jobs are far more appropriate to their nature and are far more beneficial for them.

Is a dog, consequently, the compensation for what is missing in our lives? Have we begun to substitute or replace other primary connections—with children or spouses—with our relationship with our dog, regardless of our daily routines and lifestyles? Thus, are we anthropomorphizing our canine companions right out of their proverbial fur coats? The answer to all of the above is unequivocally in the affirmative!

Grasping the basic fundamentals of dog training is no longer enough to satisfy the modern dog owner. We want it all—the dog who sits when we tell it to, and the one who sits and waits when we are not around to tell it anything.

Anyone who has ever owned a dog knows well the depth of love and attachment that instantly develops, rearranging your heart—and your life—so that neither will ever be quite the same. Gender or status have little significance on this playing field. Some of the most powerful business people in the world can literally be reduced to nail biting at the prospect of saying good-bye to a dog. Because modern dog owners bring complex needs to this relationship, we often find ourselves struggling to satisfy both the dog's and our own needs.

As a dog trainer, I can confirm that the dog's needs are quite different from ours. But as a passionate dog lover, I also find it difficult not to pull my dog onto the living room couch with the rest of the family, or set a place for him at the dinner table. Is this conflict between intellect and emotion good for the dog? Obviously not, but very few among us seem to have the willpower to say no to our dogs. Indulging a dog is a bit like loving the wrong man. You know you shouldn't be doing it, but you just can't stop yourself.

In a world where indulgence is often mistaken for love, and where dog training has become synonymous with discipline, many dog-loving people are struggling to find a balance between the kind of love that makes us feel good versus the kind of love that is good for our dogs. Add to this the fact that we now spend more and more time away from home—a separation that has a tremendously adverse effect on the ultimate behavior of our dogs—and finding the balance becomes even more difficult.

As both man and dogs' lifestyles must change with the times, so must our expectations of the behavior that results from these changes. Sometimes the solution to what appears to be a complex problem can be the subtle shifting of very basic elements. The suggestion that we all quit our jobs, relocate in what little wilderness is left in the world, and share some good, old-fashioned quality time with our dog is not exactly viable. Thus, finding a harmonious balance in the living arrangements between man and beast becomes one more burden on the "modern" dog owner. But, if our relationships with our dogs are to survive the shift into the next century, the suggestion that we conceive a better under-standing of how the dog "ticks" seems both crucial and timely.

So, who are these latchkey dogs that become psychologically unhinged the moment we kiss them good-bye each morning? Who are these dogs that have wrapped themselves so tightly around our hearts that we can hardly take a breath without it affecting both them and us? The answer might surprise you. They are city dogs and country dogs. They are large dogs and small dogs. They are retrievers, terriers, and spaniels. They are the dog next door. They are, believe it or not, your dog and my dog.

Chapter 1

Dog-Speak

What Your Dog Really Wants

If dogs could talk,
just think of the dialogue . . .
Better still, if we could speak "dog"
just think of the possibilities!

Have you ever wondered what your dog is thinking as you gaze into his eyes? What he would say if you shared a common language? You might be surprised to know that, through the language of behavior, your dog is speaking to you all the time. In fact, your own behavior around your dog might be dramatically different if you were aware of how the dog actually interpreted that behavior.

Why do some dogs chase cars? Why are others unable to resist a bite of an unsuspecting passerby? Why are some dogs antisocial and others social butterflies and why, while you are at the office earning the money to pay for your new sofa, is your dog consuming that sofa for lunch? However aggravating dog behavior can be, giving the dog away and starting over with a different one is not the answer. The answer lies in understanding the dog you have. It might surprise you to know that many of the dog's behavioral problems are not necessarily the result of poor breeding but, rather, environmental conditioning. So much of what we disapprove of in our own dog's behavior is, in fact, behavior that we are responsible for cultivating. Awareness of a few essential facts about dogs and their thinking can ultimately speak volumes to you as a dog owner.

Dog-speak occurs when you understand your dog and you've taught your dog to understand you. Knowing how to "speak dog" is the key to interpreting your dog's behavior; learning how to do so becomes the key to modifying that behavior. Surprisingly, learning dog-speak does not require life changes; it requires a change in perspective. More simply put, you don't have to become a dog, you just have to learn to think like one.

If your dog could speak to you, he would say much the same things as a human child: Please let me know where my boundaries are. Just how far can I push this issue? I'm not biting you, I'm just trying to get your attention. And the list goes on.

The issues surrounding the introduction of a new dog into one's home are much the same as welcoming home a new baby. Our relationships with our dogs—regardless of their age—are based on two fundamental concepts. First, a determination of what is needed to sustain the creature's life; second, what is needed to sustain the creature's well-being. Without an understanding of both basic principals, neither the animal nor the relationship can possibly thrive. Assuming that, prior to bringing the dog home, you have purchased a bag of dog food and have a bowl filled with clean water, you already know what is needed to sustain life. But understanding what is needed to sustain well-being, now that can be an entirely different proposition. This is where dog-speak comes in.

To begin with, dogs are "pack" animals. A pack refers to a dog's immediate family or social circle. A hierarchical order exists within this social circle that determines the dog's (as well as every other pack member's) behavior. Without a leader, there can be no followers; without rules, there can be no order. So, it's not so much the family you belong to that matters as much as how the family members behave toward each other that really counts. This is the single most important element of understanding dog behavior. Knowing this, and only this, will change the way you "parent" your dog and will instantly make you a better dog owner. The alternative—not accepting that your dog thinks and needs to live like a dog—is simply poor dog "parenting."

Another important piece of information is that dogs are signal-oriented creatures. This means that they communicate through body language as well as tones of sound. Your physical reactions to their conduct, coupled with your tone of voice, are being interpreted through the main frame of your dog's mind at all times. Understanding that your tone of voice and body language are just as important as words themselves prevents you from assuming that your dog is getting a clear signal from your words, when, in fact, he's paying attention to another message altogether from your body language. For example, if your dog is jumping up on you and your response is to gently tell him "off" at the same time as petting him, the "off" command, instead of being a correction, becomes a reward that the dog will then seek out. The result is a dog who continues to jump and a frustrated owner who continues to be jumped on. So, remember, if you send a message with a word, be sure to communicate the same message with your tone of voice and body movements.

Dogs are also "den" animals. The den refers to a dog's resting or living place. Ideally, it is a dimly lit space that has at least one opaque corner and an opening with the greatest vantage point of the rest of the dog's living space. In order for the dog to feel secure, the den should be large enough for a dog to stand up, turn around, lie down, and stretch out in. Dogs feel vulnerable in wide-open spaces and are clearly trying to send messages of stress when looking for a place to hide. This is why your dog prefers resting under the coffee table, wedging himself under your bed, or lying next to a wall, as opposed to resting in the middle of the living room. Crates or covered cages make wonderful pseudo dens and every self-respecting dog should have one.

Two more pieces of information will prove invaluable in your mastering the technique of dog-speak. Dogs think, for the most part, in the present tense. You are at a great advantage knowing that you can only modify behavior that you witness. Having a lengthy discussion about mistakes made in your absence (i.e., soiling the house, destroying furniture, constant barking, etc.) is a waste of time. So, if your dog is having trouble while your back is turned, keep a sharp eye when you are around and respond accordingly. And last, but of equal importance, keep it simple. Try to think of behavior as being either black (not acceptable) or white (acceptable). If the dog is not allowed on the furniture but he does look awfully cute up there, this becomes a gray area that the dog does not understand. He is either allowed up or he is not. Dogs learn quickly, so befuddling behavior with emotions only muddles the dog's grasp of the rules you ultimately expect him to follow. If, however, you absolutely cannot live with the thought of your precious pup on the floor and you just have to bring him up on the furniture, at the very least make it a reward for a completed task. Dogs are serious about being working members of their own pack, so even a simple "sit" becomes legitimate work and the reward can be an invitation to climb onto your favorite chair.

Now that we know the fundamentals of how dogs think, how then do we establish a common language with which to actually speak to our dogs? It's called "basic obedience," and it is the Rosetta stone of all canine/human relationships. Sharing some common words with a dog gives you the power to help the dog communicate in a language you can both understand. Without a direct line of communication to your dog, life becomes a series of guessing games and confusion for you and the dog. Imagine, for a moment, that you are in a foreign country and do not speak a word of the native tongue. With little but the art of mime, you feel lost and insecure because you do not have a mutual means of communication. If, however, you shared just a few fundamental words (i.e., "how much?" "which way," "where's the bathroom?"), you could confidently explore and enjoy your surroundings. Words become keys to otherwise locked doors. They can also function as a safety net in potentially dangerous situations (i.e., "look out," "stop," "help," "wait," "leave it," "drop," "stay").

By teaching your dog to understand the meaning of a few simple words, an entire world of possibilities opens to both dog and owner. Without basic obedience, effective communication is impossible. So, by teaching your dog that "sit" means to place its rear squarely on the ground, and "down" means to flatten its whole body on the ground, or that "off" means to get off whatever it is on and "stay" means to not move, then you can speak to your dog and your dog can understand. Believe it or not, your dog will actually enjoy understanding what you want. One of the biggest misconceptions we have of our dogs is that they will love us less if we tell them what to do. The truth is the opposite. In fact, the failure to teach a dog what you expect borders on abuse. The dog's not knowing what you want could ultimately lead to the destruction of the entire relationship. So, why not look at basic training as the key to dog-speak and a well-behaved dog simply as an added benefit of communication?

Keep in mind, too, that dogs have highly sensitive senses of smell, hearing, and sight. Telling your dog to obey a command while on a busy street or even in your living room while the television is blaring can, to a dog, constitute sensory overload. Helping and teaching your dog to shut out the rest of the world and focus on you is a task well worth the effort. Addressing your dog by name before any dialogue begins will not only redirect the dog's attention to you, but will also prepare the dog for the task. Simple changes in your perception of the dog can make a world of difference in the dog's ultimate behavior.

Think about this: If you knew that your dog viewed your physical departure as a direct threat to his survival, would you still leave him? Given most people's responsibilities, you'd have little choice. You might, however, take your leave of your pet a little differently. This may seem counterintuitive to you, but nonetheless it's true: As pack animals, dogs hunt, play, eat, and sleep together and it is specifically in their "togetherness" that they find their strength. If the "togetherness," or physical unity of the pack, is threatened by fragmentation, each dog feels weaker and more insecure.

Dogs do not consider why the group is no longer together (for example, you have to leave for the office); all they know is that they feel better and stronger when joined with their pack. We humans, however, spend a good deal of our daily lives outside the family nucleus, so leaving or separating is as much a part of our daily routine as being together. Consequently, when dogs (who are group animals leading two-dimensional lives) and humans (who are independent creatures leading three-dimensional lives) share the same pack, the "comings" and "goings" of the humans' routine can be quite stressful for the dog. Once you understand this dynamic, you can simply teach a dog that your leaving is both temporary and as integral to the daily routine as your arrival home. If you're wondering how this may be accomplished, just think of two words: "basic obedience."

By teaching the dog some basic commands, like "settle down" (relax in the down position) and "stay" (hold still) when you leave a room, you teach him that he can "stay" (hold still) when you are absent. Once the dog learns that when you leave, he "stays" or "settles down," and when you return activity resumes again, your leaving—now a routine with rules—should not alarm him at all. In fact, on the contrary—the dog will relax while you are away because your conditioning has convinced him that when he relaxes, you come back.

Thus, if you arrive home to find your furniture destroyed, you will naturally understand (because of your fluency in dog-speak) that in the dog's frenzy to find you, he simply wrecked a few things—a minor detail in a major misunderstanding. This is a simple case of healthy, intuitive canine conduct enacted upon your favorite chair. That's dog-speak and it can be applied to any living situation. So, if your dog is chasing cars, the cause may simply be a genetic predisposition (i.e., herding dogs are supposed to chase moving things); however, it might also be your daily game of tug-of-war that is teaching him to pursue and grab anything that moves through his line of vision. If your dog is a bully on-leash but a sweetheart off-leash, he may be trying to let you know that not only is your pack in need of some strong leadership, but that he has just appointed himself top dog. Or, if your dog is sick to his stomach every time you go for a ride in the car, maybe this dog can't handle being tossed about and thrown off balance. Try harnessing him in, face forward, and he might just feel better. Dogs are always trying to tell us what they want and we, as their caretakers, are often better served in terms of getting what we want when we pay attention to what they're trying to tell us.

Although we domesticated the dog many thousands of years ago, its strong ancestral instincts remain very much intact. Just beneath the surface of any dog (regardless of the specific breed) lies a wolf in sheep's clothing. If you apply the technique of dog-speak, you can communicate with the wolf while adoring the sheep. I sometimes can't help but notice a dog and dog owner struggling with each other on the street—one pulling in one direction and the other pulling in another direction, both standing firm for their own cause. The picture that is often in my mind's eye is of both man and dog down on their knees, with paws and arms respectively outstretched to the heavens, simultaneously screaming at the other: "Tell me what you want!"

"So, Tell Me What You Want, What You Really, Really Want . . ."

How does a person who clearly loves his dog end up despising that dog's behavior, and, as too often follows, despising that dog? Frequently, it is simply the absence of a common language that causes endless power struggles and frustration. This situation, while difficult, is never hopeless. By establishing some common ground (via basic obedience), people and dogs can communicate. You do not have to have a degree in animal behavior to be able to successfully determine the solution to a dog's behavioral problems. If your child was constantly acting out, wouldn't you assume that something was wrong within the infrastructure of that child's life? Well, by the same reasoning, if your dog is acting out, you may also assume that something is wrong within the infrastructure of that dog's life.

This premise is simple enough to grasp. Unfortunately, it leads us to wonder whether it is we who are actually teaching or conditioning our dogs to misbehave. Is it possible that, by misinterpreting their messages to us in the first place and then responding inappropriately, we are teaching them to behave in ever worsening ways? If your dog is destroying your property, do not necessarily assume that the dog is destructive. Disturbing canine behavior is the result of something, not the cause. If your dog is expected to lie around day after day, with little or no daily exercise as a release for stored-up energy, the destructive behavior might just be an expression of this pent-up energy. If you don't want your property destroyed, something as simple as increased daily exercise might be the solution to the problem. By the same token, if your dog barks for hours at a time whenever you leave it alone, the dog might be having trouble separating from you. Exercising and socializing this dog while building his confidence, with shorter doses of separation as well as quiet, uneventful greetings, might convince him that being alone is a momentary thing and is not a long-term nightmare.

Research has shown us that dogs are social creatures that seldom survive when alone. The fact is, without a common means of communication between you and your dog, the dog actually *is* alone—alone in his struggle to interpret messages you might not even realize you're sending.

With little time for luxuries such as staying home and curling up by the fire, modern man and his dog have misplaced their time-honored ability to communicate. With day care and day camp, sitters and walkers, behaviorists and trainers, the modern dog is taking an evolutionary leap, right over the edge of a cliff. With so many health experts today telling us to simplify, simplify, simplify, shouldn't the same hold true for our relationships with our dogs?

Imagine for a moment that your dog could speak to you. The first thing he might tell you to do would be to"sit" and "stay"! But now that you know dog-speak, you know it's okay to teach him to "settle down" and wait.

So, if the dog next door comes when he is called and your dog comes when he is good and ready, or if your friend's dog is invited to spend the summer at the beach house while your (not so perfect) dog has to stay behind in a kennel, or if you long to play Frisbee in the park with your dog but you can't get the dog to give the Frisbee back, you simply need a refresher lesson in dog-speak.

As they have proved time and again over the last several thousand years, dogs are very eager to please their human companions. Allowing yourself to think your dog's behavior is born out of spite is simply a waste of time and energy. If your dog is misbehaving, check your dog-speak skills and see what's really going on. Don't be surprised if your dog is simply trying to tell you what he wants. In a perfect world, man and dog would share the same native tongue, but until then, let's all try to increase our fluency in dog-speak.

Chapter 2

Role over Rover

Understanding Pack Dynamics

*It seems that our answer to filling certain voids in our
own lives has begun to take on the shape of a dog. . . .*

One day last summer I was window-shopping in a small, upscale,
suburban town on Long Island. As I walked down the main street, I spotted
a lovely outdoor café. I noticed a woman preparing to leave one of the outside tables. She started to walk in my direction, and I could see that she
had a Snugli strapped to her chest and in it was a baby small enough to still
be considered a newborn. As a mother of two, I cannot resist a peek at
someone else's "little miracle." I slowed my pace and craned my neck a

bit as she went by. To my surprise (but not astonishment), the "baby" was not a human baby at all. It was a puppy! A beautiful, furry, panting, adorable baby dog. I was instantly filled with "mother envy." Because I sometimes wish I might have another child, the picture of that puppy stayed in my mind's eye for most of that day. When my husband arrived home that evening, I couldn't wait to tell him that I had figured out the most perfect way for us to have another baby: "Let's just get a puppy!"

This may seem like an endearing story at first but, the truth is, more and more we are turning to dogs as a means to fill certain voids in our lives. Children, grandchildren, and primary relationships are just some of the roles we are asking our dogs to play. While loving a dog can never be perceived as inappropriate, sometimes the way in which we are loving our dogs has begun to straddle the boundary between love and need. While it is true that in some circumstances a dog is the perfect companion, the experience of dog ownership is not without its drawbacks. Anyone who has ever owned a dog will testify to the difficulty of keeping the human/dog relationship in perspective. Take one long, uninterrupted, meaningful look into the eyes of a dog and it may feel as though your soul, from then on, belongs to that dog.

There are no formal prerequisites for dog ownership. People have all kinds of individual reasons—whether born out of need or desire—for wanting to live with a dog. For centuries, the definition of need was simple: Dogs were workers and man had plenty of work. Obviously, today our relationships with our dogs are far more complicated. With women and men increasingly following life-consuming career paths, having children has become just one of many delayed priorities. With more time being spent at the office and less on a social life, finding a partner can prove as difficult as taking on a second career. Not surprisingly, the result is a large number of people without "significant others" and with very little free time who feel unfulfilled on a personal level. This is where the dog comes in.

Having already proved themselves to be therapeutic on many levels, dogs can also instantly fill the empty spaces in our lives. Not only is this immediately gratifying, but a relationship with a dog can be far less difficult and baffling than those we attempt with our own species. How-

ever, trying to satisfy the need for human interaction with a canine substitute can create many more problems than it solves. When a dog is
miscast in a human role, problems tend to be the result.

Take the single woman who's decided to get a dog for companionship. She chooses the biggest, most attractive, machismo male puppy
she can wrap her arms around and begins what she thinks is the harmless love affair between woman and dog. Day after day, they stroll in the
park enjoying the bliss of total commitment. Night after night they sleep
side by side. (After all, who better to curl up in bed with than your dog?)
Then one day it happens. A new Prince Charming enters the picture,
only this time the prince is human, and it's "role" over, Rover. But
Rover isn't about to give up his woman or his pillow and, with this, the
games begin!

Or consider the couple who decides to "have a puppy" as a step
before having a baby. I must confess I was guilty of this one myself. The
couple is feeling the need to expand their family but they are not quite
ready for the real thing. A puppy can satisfy their desire to care for and
shape another being. He is beautiful, bright, and obedient. And best of
all, they can put him in his crate and still go out to dinner and a movie
without having to hire a baby-sitter. Mom, Dad, and canine baby are the
picture-perfect family—at least for now. But sooner or later the "real"
baby arrives. Suddenly, Spot is no longer the apple of Dad's eye and
Mom no longer has the time or the energy to devote to the dog (not to
mention how Grandma feels about dog slobber all over the new baby).
Spot is expected to instantly shift roles and become the family dog. If
only it were that easy. Just as your human child would experience the
anguish caused by a new "babe" in Mom's arms, so might your miscast
canine child. Just as with the arrival of a second human child, life as an
"only child" will never be the same again. In multiple-child households,
sibling rivalry is to be expected, regardless of the species of the children.

Allowing or expecting a dog to take on a human role is not only confusing for the dog, but unnatural as well. The dog becomes conditioned
to being treated a certain (human) way until the point at which our
lifestyles—and priorities—change, a change that the dog simply does not
understand.

Dogs place a great deal of importance on "pack order," specifically, where they belong within the framework of their own group. Not only does this order settle internal disputes but it also provides a behavioral job description for each pack member. Without pack order, no one in the pack would know exactly how to behave—much like a football team that doesn't assign specific positions to its players. Just as each play would be impossible to execute because no one on the team knows where they belong or exactly what's expected of them, so would the pack be thrown into chaos and confusion. Even the simplest "play" would be nearly impossible to complete successfully.

Now, imagine the team on which each player is assigned a specific position. Under these circumstances, even the most difficult play can be carried out efficiently. Specifying who goes where and who does what gives each player the opportunity to perfect his own skills while simultaneously helping the team as a whole. A dog pack is not unlike a football team, and its dynamics are very much like those laid out in the players' handbook of rules. Once a dog's place within the pack has been established, the dog regards his role very seriously and works hard to hold on to that position. Considering the time and effort involved in becoming good at and secure in its position, asking your dog to change positions "mid-play" is not only difficult for the dog, but can have disastrous results for the whole team.

Since dogs are pack animals, and the order of hierarchy within the pack is essential to their well-being, dogs become highly stressed and confused when allowed or required to cross power boundaries. In order to raise a psychologically healthy dog one must, above all, remain conscious of the fact that your dog is just that: a dog. Asking your dog to be a human substitute becomes nothing less than a recipe for disaster.

Macho, Macho Dog . . .

Polly and Jack were the perfect "couple." A single woman with a thriving career, Polly worked long hours and had little time for a social life. Every evening, when her workday was over, she rushed home to be with Jack, a two-year-old shepherd/rottweiler mix whom Polly had adopted when he was about ten weeks old. When Polly chose him at a local shelter, she knew only that she wanted a male puppy but, after a quick inspection, she instantly picked the largest and most outgoing of the three males that were available for adoption.

Polly took Jack for long walks each evening and spent all of her spare time with him. At night Jack dutifully slept at Polly's side. Jack was, by all accounts, the perfect companion. Polly even nicknamed him "Boyfriend."

Because Jack was always at home waiting, going out socially became a rarity for Polly, and renting a movie easier than going out to one. Polly thought that she had been lucky with Jack. She had heard so many awful stories of dogs who were left alone all day and had literally destroyed the house while waiting for their owners to return. Jack, however, was an angel—he was never destructive and never acted out while Polly was away.

Then, after several months of leaving the house for little else but work, Polly accepted a dinner invitation from a man she had recently met. She and the man hit it off immediately and their relationship quickly blossomed. Paul (the human boyfriend) loved dogs and Polly couldn't wait to introduce him to Jack (the dog boyfriend). The initial meeting was promising. Paul brought a chew toy for Jack and the three went for a long walk in the neighborhood park. After several hours of ball tossing and tug-of-war, they headed home, deposited Jack in the house, and Polly and Paul went out to dinner. Jack promptly set out to "mark" his territory.

When they returned, the house reeked of a pungent odor. Jack, it seemed, had urinated all over the inside of the front door. Paul instantly scolded Jack and he slunk away in shame. Polly thought it was best that Paul leave, although they made plans for him to return the following day. Sure enough, the following day, Jack urinated on the front door again.

As Paul's visits became more frequent, Jack's behavior became more intolerable. He began to follow Polly from room to room, never letting her out of his sight. If she sat down, he practically threw himself over her feet. The only time he left her side was when Paul was there. If Paul was in the house, Jack would change his focus from Polly to Paul, following the man more like a shadow than a dog. Polly commented that even the look in Jack's eyes had changed. Whenever Paul used the bathroom, Jack sat by the door and waited. When Paul exited the bathroom, Jack immediately entered it and urinated on the toilet.

Things went from bad to worse. Whenever the couple became intimate, the dog would sit at the foot of the bed and stare at them. Eventually, when the "show" of intimacy became unbearable for him, he would begin to growl, a low, deep, agonizing sort of growl. Polly would then, of course, drag the dog off the bed and into the living room, shutting the door on her way back into her (and Jack's) bedroom. Finally, one evening when Paul was getting ready to climb into Polly (and Jack's) bed, the dog met him face-to-face and snapped at the man's cheek. The wound required only four stitches, but the relationship could not be mended. Paul and Polly decided to call it quits. Jack (the dog boyfriend) stopped his "bizarre" behavior just after Paul (the human boyfriend) packed his things and left.

How could the behavior of her wonderful dog change so drastically and so quickly? To begin with, when Polly adopted Jack, she immediately allowed (and in some ways even expected) the dog to fill the "alpha" male position in their pack. Alpha or "top" dogs assume a great amount of power within the structure of the group that they are a part of. They become responsible for the care of that group and perceive any newcomer not as a visitor but, instead, as a challenger.

Polly and Jack had lived together as a viable pack and had developed a behavioral routine that the dog and the woman began to rely on. When, however, the woman met the "real man," the routine began to change. But Polly's allowing Jack to be her pseudo mate or boyfriend sent a message to the dog that any other male was a direct challenge to his relationship with her (the alpha female), thus threatening their perfect "pack of two." Because dogs "claim" territory by marking it with their own urine or scent, Jack was merely signing his name to what he felt was rightfully his. Jack's behavior, as appalling as it might seem, was simply a normal canine response to the introduction of a new pack member. Dogs do not just roll over and give up their rank in the pack because we have suddenly changed our social priorities or interests. Any newcomer must "win" a place in the pack by first proving he is stronger, and therefore entitled to that position. Then and only then will a dog step down and relinquish his place to a newcomer. To say that dogs perceive this responsibility as stressful is to greatly understate the case.

Had Polly, from the beginning of her relationship with Jack, been more realistic as well as more careful in not allowing the dog to become a substitute man, she might have entered into and sustained her relationship with Paul with far better results. Instead, the dog's behavior ruined any chance for that relationship—and possibly any future relationships Polly might desire—to survive. Knowing that a dog is unequipped to play a human role can only help you help the dog to find its proper place in your family. Remembering that indulging the dog ultimately means confusing the dog will help you resist any temptation to substitute your dog for a surrogate human partner.

To address this problem, Polly has since enrolled in a local canine obedience class. She has learned the importance of constantly reminding the dog that there is only one alpha in their house, and that that alpha is Polly. Jack no longer sleeps in Polly's bed; instead, he sleeps on a pillow on the floor at the foot of her bed and, twice a week, outside her bedroom. She introduces Jack to any new male friend outside the house (on neutral territory) in order to help eliminate the threat of another challenge. Whenever Polly does have a friend visit, she commands Jack to "go to his place" and "down-stay" for at least five minutes. Jack not only does not mind the new "house rules" but is, in fact, relieved by no longer having to bear the responsibility of being the top dog. Everyone—but especially the dog— is considerably more at ease.

The transition that a dog makes from its dog pack to a human pack can and should be done as naturally as possible. Because a dog, when it comes to live with a human family, does not perceive itself as human at all but, rather, simply as a new pack member, understanding the dynamics of the pack plays a crucial role in understanding—and shaping—the dog's overall behavior.

Each pack is made up of essentially three segments—top, middle, and lower. The pecking order is determined by physical as well as intellectual strength. A dog does not necessarily care where in the pack its position lies as long as that position remains constant or unchallenged. It is only when we allow a dog to cross boundaries and become a top-ranking member of a human pack that the dog experiences unbearable anxiety. So, if you treat your dog like a human one day and like a dog the next, the dog is perpetually confused about his place in his own pack and, thus, feels that he has to constantly prove his strength. Talk about stress inducing!

The moment a puppy enters the world, its first real job is to find its own place among its dog pack members. The same is instinctively true for it when it comes to live with a human family. Since everybody naturally wants to be a king and not a pawn, the dog's first instinct as a newcomer is to try for the top-dog spot. As adorable as this behavior can initially seem, fostering it is not only confusing but can eventually be disastrous. For with power comes responsibility as well as privilege, and it is the top dog that is responsible for the sustenance of the entire pack.

From the time man first domesticated the dog, he has known that a dog's place with him was as a worker, not a leader. Because dogs are incapable of overseeing the overall well-being of humans, it becomes the humans' job to oversee the well-being of the dog. To put it simply: Dogs want and need to be constantly reminded that they are dogs.

"Oh, Baby, Baby It's a Wild World . . ."

From the moment the pregnancy test read positive, Janet and Steven had mixed emotions. They were over the top about the prospect of having a baby but, frankly, they were afraid of what it might do to the dog. They had always known the day would come when they would start a "real" family, but it was hard to believe that six years had passed since they had first brought home their adorable "baby girl" puppy. Tiffany was the apple of their eye and spoiling her over the last few years had been so easy, so natural . . . she was just so cute. Tiffany is an American Staffordshire bull terrier, or American pit bull terrier, as they are often referred to.

When Janet and Steven decided to adopt Tiffany, they were not unaware of the special needs of her particular breed. They researched her ancestry and knew that her breeding was quite sound. They also knew that training was essential for this kind of dog, so Steven took her twice a week to obedience class, which they both came through with flying colors. Both Janet and Steven were careful to keep Tiffany on a leash whenever they were out for daily walks. They took offense whenever someone commented about Tiffany's breed and felt badly that anyone could actually be afraid of their sweet dog.

As the months passed, Janet and Steven fell more and more in love with their dog. In fact, they searched high and low for outdoor cafés, dog-friendly parks, and just about any social activity that included dogs. At night they would, all three, curl up on the sofa and watch TV. Tiffany loved any kind of dog treat, so Janet always kept a pocketful just in case her "baby girl" wanted a snack. The idea of Tiffany sleeping on the floor seemed outrageous so, of course, she slept right between her "parents." If the dog seemed restless at night, Janet would rock her in her arms and stroke her until she fell asleep.

Tiffany's food dish was always full, and if she didn't seem enthusiastic about its contents, Janet would coax her to eat by hand-feeding her. Toys littered the floor of the house. Not just dog toys—Tiffany loved Beanie Babies and plush stuffed toys as well. Whenever the couple were both at home, they played a routine game that they aptly called "mommy loves you," "daddy loves you." Janet would sit at one end of the couch with a dog treat and Steven (also with a treat) would sit at the other. On the "go" signal, Janet and Steven would simultaneously chant "mommy loves you," "daddy loves you." The chanting continued until the dog chose either the man or the woman. Whoever Tiffany ran to and grabbed the treat from first was the winner. Laying this kind of behavioral foundation for any youngster would be precarious, but when that youngster is a dog, look out!

Tiffany grew so used to her indulgent lifestyle that she would go so far as jumping on the dining room table to pluck a morsel off any plate she chose. Steven and Janet knew that the behavior was a bit "over the top," but they didn't really mind because Tiffany was, after all, "family."

It wasn't until the "real" baby arrived that the inevitable happened. Janet and Steven had no idea how much time and energy a human baby required, and they also had no idea just how much they would want to protect this new baby. Life in Janet, Steven, and Tiffany's home changed in an instant. The couple still adored their dog but no longer had the time or the energy to treat her as they always had. Tiffany, on the other hand, had no idea that she was a dog.

With the addition of the new baby, the idea of the dog sleeping in their bed suddenly seemed outrageous. Tiffany was relegated to sleeping on the floor. All old plush toys were thrown away because they were full of "dog" germs and all new plush toys were off-limits to Tiffany because they belonged to the new baby. Whenever Janet left the house, she no longer took Tiffany with her—instead, she took the new baby. Tiffany became confused and stressed. Her once "adorable" behavior was now being viewed as obnoxious. But she was only doing what she had been conditioned to do all of her life. Consequently, she tried all her old "tricks," but Steven and Janet turned a deaf ear. What was she doing wrong? All attempts to get the attention she was so accustomed to having failed thus far, Tiffany decided to try some new behavior.

Whether left alone or in a room filled with people, Tiffany began to bark obsessively. This upset Janet enormously. She began to lock the dog in a spare bedroom to muffle the noise. The barking got worse. Dogs are often instinctively very protective of babies and Tiffany kept a close watch on the baby. Steven became concerned about the baby and the dog being face-to-face on the floor so, whenever the baby was crawling about, the dog was gated in the kitchen. Tiffany was allowed out, however, when the baby was in her swing, but the dog watched the baby intently. This made Janet very nervous. She was certain that Tiffany disliked the baby. After all, the dog's behavior had changed almost immediately after the baby had arrived.

A few weeks later, while the baby was eating in her high chair, Tiffany jumped up and grabbed a piece of food from the tray—mirroring her previous (permitted) behavior at the dining room table. The dog accidentally nipped one of the baby's fingers, an event that confirmed Janet's fears. She was certain that Tiffany was "out to get" the baby! After anguishing over what to do next, Steven's father offered to take Tiffany to live with him. Now the dog sees Janet, Steven, and the baby twice a year, when they visit Steven's father.

Believe it or not, Tiffany's fate is more common than any dog lover would like to admit. Hundreds of thousands of dogs begin their lives as somebody's first "child," only to end up as a disjointed member of an extended family or, even worse, no longer a member of that family at all. Rather than suggesting that there be a limit to the love one feels for a dog, a better suggestion would be that we attempt to realistically define our devotion to our dog—out of compassion for and an understanding of the dog itself. Don't love your dog any less, just be careful about your ultimate expectations of that love. Because Tiffany had initially been rewarded for inappropriate behavior with her "parents' " love, it was only natural that she continue to behave inappropriately even after Janet and Steven no longer found such behavior acceptable. If a specific behavior has always earned your dog affection, changing that behavior (because it is no longer desirable) does not come easily to the dog. Still, with effort, this behavior can be modified.

Life changes don't always come with the advantage of a warning. Having a baby, however, happens to be one change that does afford the luxury of (on average) nine months of planning. If your "first born" is a dog and your family is about to expand, easing the dog into its new role as the dog does not always have to be traumatic or painful. Start by imagining that the (human) baby is already living in your home. If you don't think you want the dog jumping up on a bed that a baby is lying on, make the bed (or any other furniture) off-limits now, before the real baby arrives. Don't wait for the moment the baby moves in or the dog might associate the change with that baby. Start to treat the dog as if not only an infant baby, but a baby in many different stages of growth, lives in your house. Gently approach the dog during mealtime and slowly drop a biscuit into the dog's food bowl. Then, touch various parts of the dog's body (i.e., tail, back legs, rear end, etc.) to desensitize him while he is eating. The split second he turns to look at you, praise him and give him another biscuit or treat. He will soon learn to tolerate your bothering him while he is eating and to associate being approached while eating as a pleasant break for a reward (i.e., the treat). This way, when the baby begins to grow and explore the dog's feeding area, the dog is already used to having his feeding area explored. Now, a few weeks before the baby is born, bring a doll (preferably one that makes crying and cooing noises) into the house.

Treat the doll as you would treat the new baby and allow the dog plenty of time to get used to you with something in your arms. If the dog treats the doll inappropriately, correct the behavior and, if the dog treats the doll gently, praise accordingly. This kind of exposure can prove invaluable for the dog and the family. Knowing how a dog is going to respond beforehand both gives you plenty of time to modify unwanted behavior and gives the dog plenty of time to adjust to his new role. At the time of the blessed event, try to remember to save a receiving blanket that has been used to wipe off the baby and send it home to the dog. It might sound rather repulsive to you, but the smells on the blanket will allow the dog to become familiar with the baby's scent. When you arrive home with the baby, the dog will already be comfortable with the "new pack member's" smell. In situations such as these, a little foresight can go a long way.

As with any dog, regardless of life changes, the knowledge and practice of basic obedience is a must. Without even a few basic commands (i.e., "wait," "off," "down," "stay," "easy," "leave it," etc.), sending messages to the dog about his behavior is virtually impossible. If you can't communicate with him now, how can you possibly communicate with him when he is right in the middle of a life change? So, if you're planning a change—whether in family size or geography or office hours—that's going to affect your dog (and that includes any change), a refresher course in basic obedience is an absolute must. Just as people go through behavioral changes as they experience life changes, so do dogs. One of the great advantages of being human is that we are able to apply our powers of reasoning to those life changes, something your dog, in contrast, cannot do. While it is never a good idea to assimilate your dog into a human role, if you have already done so and would like to set things straight, you can help your dog to make the transition easily. Doing so will save everyone involved, but especially the dog, a lot of suffering. When a person decides to adopt a dog, it is likely that some thought about what is ultimately expected of that dog has occurred. Thus, this thoughtful person begins immediately to lay the foundation for what he expects of his dog's behavior. If you suspect you would detest living with a spoiled child, be careful not to cultivate that sort of behavior in your dog. If you think you might want a real child, be very careful not to raise the dog as an "only child." And, if you are searching for your one true soul mate and decide to temporarily designate the dog as that, be aware that switching partners down the road can be a great deal messier than divorce court.

A dog is never unhappy being a dog; in fact, it is a far easier job than that of any human. It is only when we inappropriately elevate the status of our dogs to that of humans that we unwittingly transfer human responsibilities to that dog as well. A dog is not emotionally equipped to handle human responsibilities. Perhaps, when we live with dogs, we have no choice but to love them, and this can cause our judgment to be clouded. Whatever our reasons, for the dog the result is always damaging.

Without warning or proper behavior modification, dogs don't willingly shift their position in the pack. Since a dog's role, ultimately, defines his rank and power within his pack, switching roles can only be done by contest, not by design. So, when a dog is suddenly expected to "role" over—trust me, it is never a pretty sight!

Chapter 3

My Dog/Myself

Is Your Dog Making You Crazy or
Are You Making Your Dog Crazy?

Not every dog/person problem can be solved by modi-
fying the dog's behavior. Sometimes the person must
first seek help before the dog can be healed. . . .

D

ogs are highly sensitive, signal-oriented creatures that pick up
even the slightest inconsistency in the confidence level of another animal. Indeed, it is their keen sense of observation that has helped ensure
the survival of their species. This is illustrated by the expression you
have no doubt heard, "Dogs have a sixth sense."

Perhaps in our modern times that sixth sense is beginning to work against them. Because they are such astute observers of their surroundings, they don't miss a trick. Some people say they can even smell fear. Well, judging by their behavior, dogs can "smell" a host of psychological troubles and it is those very troubles that are now popping up all over the place, specifically in our dogs. So, we must consider whether we are naturally drawn to dogs that possess similar personality traits to our own, or whether our own personality traits—and flaws—are being unnaturally manifested in our dogs. It has long been said that dogs look like the people they live with. If that's true, then perhaps they are starting to behave like us, too. And, in that case, we had better start being more conscious of how we behave around our dogs.

To Cook or Not to Cook . . .

I received a call from a woman named Joan who was recommended to me by a local veterinarian. She said several people had told her that her Jack Russell terrier, Topper, was "out of control" and needed some "real" obedience training. She explained that whenever she left her apartment, her dog would bark obsessively and, after months of trying several behavioral-modification techniques that proved ineffective, Topper and Joan were in danger of being evicted from their home. So, after a desperate visit to her veterinarian, where she went to discuss what she thought of as the only solution left—cutting the dog's vocal chords—the vet suggested Joan call me.

When I arrived at the apartment door, Topper was making enough noise to rival a fireworks display on the Fourth of July. Without so much as a "Who is it?," the door opened and I was pulled inside. "Get in," the woman said, in a near frantic whisper. "Do you see what I mean? My neighbors are ready to kill me!"

Having dealt with this kind of audio display before, I immediately knelt down to Topper's level to put the dog at ease, all the while assuring Topper's owner that everything would be fine. Knowing full well that any movement on my part might ignite another noise explosion, I remained on the floor for several minutes until the dog was sufficiently convinced that I had come in peace.

Joan, as it turned out, was a fast-talking ball of energy who immediately declared her love for her dog and explained that she had gone, and would continue to go, to any length to help Topper with her problem. Regardless of the tension that surrounded them in their apartment building, Joan would not be separated from her companion, even if it meant having to find another place to live. As she spoke, she nervously bit what was left of the nails on every one of her ten fingers. With this information and a brief account of the dog and woman's past twelve months, it became at least partially clear to me why destiny had chosen this dog for this person. Both possessed high-strung, frenetic energy, making it (at a glance) slightly more difficult to determine in which one the anxious behavior had originated, dog or owner.

Because dogs are such astute observers of their environment and speak volumes through their own body language, as Joan and I talked, I watched Topper with a keen eye. As I sat, taking mental notes of Joan's detailed account of Topper's daily routine, I noticed the dog's eyes darting nervously back and forth, keeping an efficient eye on her owner (the center of her existence) and me (the intruder). This was a clear sign that Topper felt herself responsible for Joan's safety. I pointed this out and Joan responded by saying she thought it odd that the dog would feel responsible for her because she was careful to tend to Topper's every need. This was yet another sign that the dog was in charge.

Joan explained that she had decided to get a dog shortly after the death of her mother and had purchased the dog from a breeder at seven weeks of age. From their first days together, Topper had been Joan's closest companion. They spent as much time together as Joan's lifestyle allowed, and Joan repaid Topper's love and loyalty by indulging the dog in her every whim. Because Topper was not very social with other dogs, whenever dog and owner saw another dog in the street, Joan thought it best to keep their distance. Joan even hired a groomer to come to her apartment so the dog would not have to spend any time away from home or around other dogs. Topper did, however, love people. So whenever

Joan had plans to go out, she thought it best to invite friends to stop by the apartment first.

Joan left for work each morning at 8:35 A.M. and returned each evening by 5:25 P.M. She hired a dog walker to come at noon each day to walk Topper for thirty minutes. At the suggestion of several other dog owners, Joan also hired a well-known dog trainer to come to her home and teach Topper basic obedience. She purchased and studied the latest dog training books and subsequently had done everything she could think of to give her dog every opportunity for a full and healthy life. From Joan's account, all should have been perfect between woman and dog. So what could possibly have gone wrong?

To begin with, Joan had initially purchased her dog to fill the void in her life left by her mother's death. This is both a common and an understandable response to loss. But, all too often, when replacing a human relationship with a relationship with a dog, it instantly and falsely elevates the dog's status to that of a human—a very confusing development for a dog. A dog needs to be accepted as a working member of its family. If the dog's subordinate, working role is not clearly defined in the family, the dog instinctively tries to become that family's leader. In this particular case, Topper was clearly this family's leader. Since dogs cannot successfully run human households, allowing the dog to be in charge never ends well.

Because Jack Russell terriers have a reputation for being highstrung and feisty, Joan associated Topper's ever growing nervous and sometimes aggressive energy with a personality trait of her breed. Joan mentioned that she had only left Topper for more than a workday once each year to visit relatives in California. When she did, Joan left Topper with the trainer, whom the dog had grown quite fond of. Joan had used a crate (a cage) for the dog since the dog was a pup, so when Topper went to stay with the trainer, Joan was careful to send the crate along with her.

It had been almost forty-five minutes since I had arrived and, by now, Topper had jumped on Joan's lap and been licking her own paws (as Joan bit her nails) for what seemed like an eternity. Not once, even for a moment, during this first meeting, did the dog relax. When I asked Joan if she was aware of her dog's obsessive licking, she responded by telling me that "whenever Topper was not asleep, she was either licking her paws or licking the floors from one end of the apartment to the other."

As the conversation drifted back to why Joan had contacted me in the first place, she got up and crossed the living room (with the dog at her heels) to get herself a drink in the kitchen. Then, the most astounding thing happened. When Joan crossed the threshold to the kitchen, Topper dropped to the floor, in near paralyzed fear, and began to shake. "Don't worry," Joan said to the dog, "I'm not going to cook anything!" I was, to say the least, intrigued.

Joan explained that sometime after returning from her last trip to California, Topper had developed a fear of soup pots. It seemed that, during the dog's last stay with her trainer, the trainer had found her to be somewhat more unruly than usual. What Joan and the trainer had overlooked was that Topper's unruly behavior was clearly a symptom of separation anxiety (anxious behavior triggered or stimulated by the signals of separation).

One of the trainer's methods of getting "control" of a dog was to bang an object against a wall, making a loud noise and thereby distracting the dog and changing its focus. Clearly, a loud bang would distract anyone, so the trainer advised Joan to "bang away" if the dog became too vocal or too unruly. Joan was so eager to fix Topper that she inadvertently took the trainer's advice a bit too far.

Joan had begun to find Topper difficult and noisy whenever she was getting ready to leave for work. She remembered what the trainer had told her about getting control so, just after putting Topper in her crate and closing its door, Joan grabbed a small soup pot from the kitchen and banged it on the top of the dog's crate. This, to say the least, distracted Topper and she was instantly quiet. Wow, Joan thought, this really works!

The months that followed, Joan recounted, were nothing short of a nightmare: "Now, every time I have to go out or leave for work, she barks so hysterically that the neighbors are signing a petition to get us kicked out of the building. To make things even worse," she said, "whenever I am home, Topper never leaves my side. I can't cook a single meal, and she never stops licking the floors. Every time I reach out to hold her, she cowers and shuts her eyes as if I am going to hit her. If I didn't know better, I'd think she was afraid of ME . . ."

Joan had hit the nail on the head! The dog was afraid of her—or, more specifically, what Joan was going to do to her (i.e., slam the pot against Topper's crate). The woman was mortified—she had done nothing but love this dog. How could Topper possibly fear her?

The answer is simple. First and foremost, Joan and Topper speak two different languages. Dogs send messages through body language and tones of sound. For months, Topper had been trying to tell Joan that something was wrong with their "pack dynamics." Topper, who initially received signals from Joan that she (the dog) was clearly in charge, was unable to keep track of the subordinate pack member (Joan) every time the woman left the apartment. The dog was simply unable to deal with the stress associated with the woman leaving her. Consequently, every time Joan tried to leave the house, the dog's response was to literally cry out that their relationship just wasn't working. Topper was now clearly in the throws of full-blown separation anxiety. What started out as one problem had quickly snowballed into many.

Since the very day that Joan had brought Topper to live with her, she had treated the dog like a high-ranking member of their pack. So, naturally, the dog instinctively placed herself "in charge." Every time Joan left Topper for any reason, the dog was unable to do her job: keep track of and protect Joan.

This created, to say the least, a stressful situation for Topper. She became "a queen without a kingdom." In addition, by not socializing her with other dogs, Topper learned to rely on Joan for social stimulation as well. Whenever Joan's friends stopped by, to the woman it was healthy social exposure for her dog but, to the dog, it was a clear signal that her "charge" would be leaving, yet again. And, as icing on the cake, whenever Topper protested the separation, her most beloved partner (Joan) would put her in the one place the dog thought of as a "safe harbor" (the crate) and bang on it with a pot, turning it into a torture chamber. So, instead of trusting Joan, Topper began to fear her. What began as a single confusing signal about who was in charge had grown into quite a mixed bag. What Joan and Topper desperately needed was nothing short of a new start.

First and foremost, a clear set of rules and regulations needed to be established, both in order for the two to communicate and to clarify who was in charge of the pack. If two species are to share living space, the stronger, more intelligent species must be in charge. With the introduction of basic obedience into this mix, the hierarchical order of the household would become clear. This common language of obedience ("sit," "come," "down," "stay," "off," etc.) becomes the foundation of all control and communication in our relationships with our dogs.

Once this foundation of language was laid, Joan needed to practice and reinforce it daily so that it became part of Topper's routine. Using food as a reward helped the dog enjoy the new routine. It was not necessary for Joan to keep Topper from sharing her favorite chair or sleeping in the same bed. It was, however, imperative that Topper only be allowed these privileges if invited by Joan. Whenever Topper felt the need to be close to Joan (whether joining her on the couch or by following her around), I suggested that Joan command the dog "off" and tell her to "sit." If Topper obeyed, Joan was to praise the act and then "command" the dog to "come up." This not only reinforced Joan's status as a leader, but allowed Topper to be close to her companion as well.

This new routine was to be combined with more social time outdoors (with other dogs as well as people). I then suggested that Joan place the "dreaded" soup pot in the middle of the living room floor and put a favorite toy and a treat on top of it. She was to always quietly praise the dog for taking the treat off the pot and was to replace the treat when the spot was empty. I also suggested that Joan place a sheet on part of Topper's crate, creating a corner and a ceiling so the dog would feel as if she was in more of a "den" than a cage. I cautioned Joan to be patient as their new relationship took shape.

Happily, after a few short weeks, Topper began not only to trust Joan, but to view her as a leader. The dog was thereby relieved of the source of her stress and confusion. Whenever Joan left the apartment, Topper no longer believed she had the job of "running the show," so, like any healthy subordinate pack member, she simply rested quietly until her alpha came home. Whenever Joan was at home, she was careful always to let Topper know through the simple commands the dog had learned what behavior she considered acceptable. The barking and obsessive licking slowed to a near stop and both woman and dog were enjoying their new roles. Topper was even eating her meals out of the very soup pot that a short time before had caused her such great angst. If your dog believes himself to be in charge, any insubordination on your part becomes a direct challenge for power and any power struggle lost by the dog only strengthens his determination to climb back to the top. It is far easier not to blur power lines in the first place. Show me a leader who lives under the constant threat of a coup and I will show you a very nervous leader.

Separation anxiety is not exclusive to canines. Clearly, we as modern dog owners are having as much trouble separating from our dogs as they are now having separating from us. As difficult as it may be to admit, it is nonetheless true. No longer just cohabitating with our canines, we are fast on our way to becoming codependent with them. And it is this codependence that lies at the root of so many of our dog's behavioral problems.

Something as seemingly unimportant as the initial timing of your dog's arrival plays an integral role in the success of the overall relationship. It is only natural when getting a dog to want to spend as much time together as possible. It is even a good idea, when purchasing or adopting a dog, to do so with at least two or three days to spend helping the newcomer get adjusted to the new pack. These first few days should, however, be broken up into segments, allowing your dog the necessary time to rest, play, explore, interact, bond, and, believe it or not, be alone in order to get a healthy new start. But it is the dog's long-term daily routine that ultimately creates the psychologically sound—or unsound—dog. Therefore, it is imperative that a dog finds security in its daily routine. The moment that routine becomes a guessing game (i.e., Where are you going? When are you coming back? Are you coming back?), behavioral problems will surely ensue.

Take for instance the adopted or secondhand dog. With a behavioral history that often remains unknown, the animal comes to us with a handicap. Needier than most, it appears that the secondhand dog requires a great deal of attention in order to mend the psychological wounds of the past.

We, as dog lovers, immediately set out to disprove any doubts the dog might have about bonding with us. With great gusto, we change our schedules to reassure the dog that this time life will be different—you will never leave him. And you don't, at least for a while. You decline the dinner invitations and reason that the "hot" new movie will soon be out on video. You'd rather watch it at home curled up on the couch with the dog anyway. And, after a sweet-smelling day at the groomer, a fun-filled trip to the pet-supply store, and a whole new "leash" on life, "Fido" should be as good as new, right? Well, perhaps not.

Although our intentions are sincere, ultimately the time must and will come to separate, even if only for a short while, and Fido will most assuredly fall apart. "Where are you going?!" he might say if he came equipped with a much-needed interpreter. "Are you ever coming back?! You promised never to leave me—ever!!" And so the landslide begins.

Little does Fido know (or does he?) that you are pressed up against the other side of the front door, white-knuckled at the prospect of leaving your beloved pooch. Each hour that you are apart feels more like a month. When you finally do arrive home (anticipating a happy reunion), Fido has soiled the living room rug, shredded your favorite needlepoint pillow, and compelled several neighbors to leave messages on your answering machine regarding "all the noise!" Avoiding such a fate is actually rather simple. Just create an atmosphere in which the dog feels secure whether you're home or not.

Hold, Hold Me Tight . . .

Michael, an investment banker, spent a great deal of time at the office and was seldom home except on weekends. His family had a dog when he was growing up and his memories of that dog made him hope to someday have his own. After living on his own for several years, he felt he was prepared to take on the responsibility of a dog. As his schedule precluded getting a puppy, adopting an adult dog seemed the perfect answer. He knew he wanted a large dog, and because he spent weekends at a time-share at the beach, exercise (at least on weekends) would not be a problem. Michael believed he had thought of everything. He hired a dog walker for the midday walk and asked friends if they would stop by from time to time if he couldn't get home for the dog's evening walk. All that remained was to choose the dog.

The trip to the shelter was short and sweet. Michael knew exactly what he was looking for and the moment he saw the wagging tail and smiling face of the black Labrador retriever (named Jake), he was certain that this was the dog for him. It often happens that a person is unwittingly attracted to a specific breed of dog that requires more attention and training than the owner's lifestyle allows. But at first glance Michael and Jake were the perfect man/dog combination. Both young and athletic, Michael and Jake were an ideal energy match. The dog looked physically healthy and seemed emotionally sound. The people at the shelter told Michael that the dog had lived with a family in the suburbs since he was a puppy, and their records indicated that after the birth of their first child, Jake had become too much to handle, so they thought it best to find the dog a more appropriate home. As is often the case, that was the extent of the dog's "detailed" history. Anyhow, Michael thought the dog was beautiful, so he signed on the dotted line and took him home.

Their first days together were nothing short of perfect. They ate together, played together, and slept together. Michael had planned a few days off from work so he and Jake could get to know each other. Whenever he had somewhere to go, Michael made sure he took the dog along. Jake's first family had apparently done some basic obedience work with him because Jake was already proficient at "sit," "down," and "stay." Owning a dog, Michael thought, was easier and more rewarding than he had remembered. Everyone on the street stopped this new "team" and could not get over how well behaved this young dog was. Michael knew that he had really lucked out. What Michael didn't know was that disaster was around the corner.

As their long weekend of getting acquainted was drawing to a close, Michael began to get ready to return to work. He called the dog walker to confirm Jake's standing midday appointment. In the morning, Michael took Jake for his walk (as usual), showered (as usual), dressed (as usual), fed him (as usual), grabbed his briefcase (*not* as usual), and headed for the door without the dog (*not* as usual). At first, Jake looked puzzled but sat patiently watching Michael's every move. Michael wrote the dog walker a note, kissed the dog good-bye, explained that he would be home soon, and headed out the door. But, as the door shut, Michael felt an unusual pain in his stomach. He stood, for a second, with his head pressed against the door, trying to catch his breath. Wow, he thought, I must be coming down with the flu. Michael did not have the flu. What he was feeling was the unbearable pain of separation. From the moment the man had slipped the collar around the dog's neck for the very first time, he had doomed himself to the heart-wrenching, soul-snatching, mind-bending, all-consuming pain of separation anxiety. As the weeks passed, Michael's dream of owning his own dog seemed to be turning into nothing short of a nightmare. Leaving Jake was becoming nearly impossible. He had difficulty concentrating at the office, so preoccupied was he with getting home. He looked forward to weekends when he and Jake would run on the beach for miles and spend endless hours together playing and relaxing. He even called home several times a day and via the answering machine told the dog that he would be home as soon as he could. He canceled evening plans, and made excuses for not being his usual social self. Mornings were dragged out until the very last second, when Michael would lie on the floor with Jake and console him (or was it himself?), telling him he had no choice but to leave and go to the office. Arriving home at night, he would immediately give Jake a "treat," and shower the dog with affection. Michael thought Jake was taking their separation in stride. Other than a slight loss of appetite and some pacing throughout the night, the dog seemed unaffected by the man's departure—or so Michael believed.

Two months later, things took a turn for the worse. Michael would arrive home from the office and find an article of clothing torn up or a chair leg chewed on. He searched high and low for the television remote control and finally found remnants of it under the couch, obviously devoured by Jake. A week later, Jake consumed the answering machine. Every day, Michael repeated the morning good-bye ritual, and every day Jake continued to destroy Michael's belongings. One of Michael's coworkers suggested that the dog had too many toys to choose from, so Michael took away Jake's toys. The next day, Jake ate almost the entire kitchen table. Michael was aghast. Why would his dog—whom he had done nothing but shower with love and companionship—do such a thing? Everything between them had been perfect—hadn't it? Michael finally came to the conclusion that Jake must have been angry with him for leaving him every day so, in his anger, he destroyed the apartment.

Michael was wrong. In truth, Jake was not angry at all; he was just looking for Michael. And even more important, he was acting out a behavior that Michael had actually taught him. Given the way Michael had been behaving whenever he left the apartment—calling the answering machine each afternoon (unaware that hearing his voice made Jake even more frantic to find him), showering the dog with affection upon returning—he had basically taught Jake to feel uncomfortable without him. So, naturally, the dog began to search for him. To a dog, the first place to find something missing is in the smell of that thing. As Michael's smell was on all of his belongings, Jake began to tear at those belongings thinking that, in them, he might find Michael. Unaware of Jake's motivation, Michael continued to send inappropriate messages to Jake every time he left the apartment, and the dog continued to express his distress whenever Michael was absent. Could it be possible that Michael was actually training Jake to destroy his home? Believe it or not, yes!

The problem began the first time Michael left the dog alone. First, Michael changed the pack's routine by suddenly leaving the dog behind instead of taking him along, as usual. Naturally, the dog felt ill at ease with the new routine. Then, to make matters worse, Michael showed that he, too, was ill at ease with the new routine. As each day passed, Michael reconfirmed that leaving Jake made him uncomfortable, and communicated this discomfort to the dog. As Michael prepared to leave, Jake recognized the familiar signals and became just as uncomfortable as Michael. Believe it or not, it is much the same as teaching a dog to "sit." The dog begins to respond to signals as well as words. (For example: If you say the word "sit" while simultaneously giving a hand signal, then help the dog into a sitting position, the dog learns that whenever you say "sit," along with a hand signal, he is to get into the sitting position.) Michael's morning routine (i.e., dressing in a suit, picking up his briefcase, and lying on the floor with the dog— "signals" that he was about to leave) became the dog's signal to feel anxious as well. Jake was, in fact, a well-trained dog. But, because of Michael's conditioning, this dog (that he couldn't live without) had become the dog he couldn't live with.

So what should you do if the dog that you are crazy about is beginning to make you crazy? To begin with, don't make the same mistakes Michael did. If saying good-bye causes you distress, examine your behavior and be sure it is not affecting the dog. Avoid letting this behavior become a daily signal that something negative is about to happen. Help the dog to be more independent by making as little as possible of your leaving and returning. Be sure to enlist your dog as a working pack member, not a spoiled child. Be very careful not to encourage excessive dependence in your dog. The time will come when you must part, even for a short time, and it would be better for you and your dog if parting were not such sweet sorrow. And, if you absolutely must fall apart every time you have to leave, please don't do it in front of the dog. One more thing, turn down the volume on your answering machine!

Dogs are not born with neurotic behavior; such behavior is learned. While some canine behavior can be labeled as instinctive and/or genetic (i.e., digging, retrieving, barking, mouthing, etc.), other behavior is simply learned. Just as a dog can learn to "sit," "come," and "heel" when taught, so, too, can a dog be taught to psychologically weaken when given a signal. Would we deliberately do such a thing? Of course not. But effective dog parenting requires us to control our own behavior as well as our dog's.

Take Two and Call Me
in the Morning . . .

Linda, a receptionist in a large metropolitan law firm, had trouble making eye contact with the attorneys in her office. Linda's therapist felt she was allowing herself to be intimidated by her superiors and therefore should work on her self-esteem. She had begun to bite her nails, had trouble sitting still, and spent the day snacking on chocolate bars. She eventually began forcing herself to purge herself of her evening meal because of all the added calories from the candy. On one of her visits to her therapist, the therapist recommended that she either find a less stressful job or—because studies have shown that living with an animal helps relieve stress—get a dog. Linda opted for the dog. At first Linda felt as if she had been released from a "living hell." Once she had made the decision to get a dog, she felt a freedom that she had never known before. She had always wanted a dog but hadn't known if she could handle the responsibility. After all, her own life was in a bit of a shambles. Nonetheless, the prospect of having a dog to share her life with was exhilarating.

Finding a puppy was easy. Linda passed a pet shop each evening on her way home from work. She had always enjoyed watching the puppies in the window, dreaming of the day she might waltz into the store and buy one. On the day she entered the pet shop to actually buy one, her heart was racing a thousand miles an hour. Linda spotted a twelve-week-old bichon frise, the sweetest little ball of white curls. Her constant barking made Linda feel as if the dog were calling to her and saying, "Pick me! Pick me!" Linda instantly felt connected to this dog. So, within minutes Linda had picked the puppy, whom she named Lucy.

During the first few months, the dog seemed to be just what the doctor ordered. While at the office, Linda's thoughts were constantly with Lucy. The result of this was that work became quite a bit easier to bear. Although she still suffered from bulimia, still bit her nails, and still could not look at her superiors when they entered her work space, once at home, Linda was immensely comforted by the presence of her new roommate. Lucy had been waiting around all day and greeted Linda with such raw enthusiasm that the woman could not have felt more needed or loved. After rushing home each evening and greeting her dog, Linda would begin long, emotional monologues about her daily woes. Lucy would listen (with seeming comprehension), and suddenly the world seemed right—for Linda.

Because Lucy spent extended hours alone each day and was not a "big" dog, Linda (anxious that her dog be happy) thought the most humane thing for Lucy would be to leave "paper" on the floor to use as a bathroom. Because of this, Lucy and Linda had the option of going out only when they wanted to. They did take long walks in the evening when the weather allowed and, once home, they would have their dinner. Linda simultaneously prepared and served both of their meals, the dog on the floor and the woman at the kitchen table. It bothered Linda that her "roommate" (as she referred to the dog) ate on the floor and she often toyed with the idea of allowing Lucy to eat with her at the table: "After all, we are equals," Linda thought, "and what's good enough for me is good enough for my dog." After eating, Lucy would follow Linda into the bathroom and watch while Linda vomited up her evening meal. The woman's weekly discussions with her therapist were becoming less about her and more about the dog. Linda's compulsive behavior was far from under control, but talking about Lucy was much more pleasant. The transformation was gradual, but after about a year, Linda's neighbors began to complain that Lucy's barking had become almost constant throughout the day. Linda knew that her dog was pretty "vocal" (that was clear from their first meeting at the pet shop), but she assumed that the dog's barking stopped shortly after she'd left for work. She also thought the "scratches on the floor," just inside the front door, were just Lucy's way of saying she wanted to leave with Linda. However, one evening Linda arrived home and noticed that Lucy had vomited up her breakfast. Linda was concerned that Lucy might be sick so she took her to the vet. The veterinarian eased the woman's concerns by explaining that some dogs just eat very quickly. Vomiting now and then would surely not prove fatal. But, after weeks of coming home to Lucy's breakfast regurgitated on the kitchen floor, Linda did become concerned. After a series of tests confirmed that nothing was physically wrong with Lucy, Linda was in a near hysterical state about Lucy's well-being. With nowhere left to turn, Linda naturally discussed Lucy's "problem" with her therapist. The therapist replied (albeit jokingly), "Linda, Lucy's behavior is beginning to sound just like yours!"

As strange as this may sound; the therapist was, in fact, correct. There was nothing physically wrong with Lucy at all; the dog's problems were emotional. Just as Linda experienced the pressures of her days (and chose to relieve those pressures by biting her nails and vomiting), so Lucy was feeling the pressures of her own existence. But more important, Lucy had begun to mimic Linda's stress-relieving behavior. Dogs are unequipped to understand the complexities of human behavior but intuitive enough to attempt to copy it. Considering the reasons Linda chose to get a dog in the first place, one might conclude that Lucy was purchased almost as a prescription drug. After all, Linda's therapist did prescribe that Linda get a dog. This is not to suggest that Linda didn't love her dog completely, but the ways in which Linda mistook need for love ultimately got them into a mess. And what a mess this was.

In order to help Lucy, Linda had no choice but to help herself. Because she so desperately loved her dog, she found it easier to change her own behavior once she understood that Lucy's health was contingent on her own. Understanding that dogs are signal-oriented creatures who rely on consistent behavior as a springboard for their own, Linda began to resist sending the wrong signals to Lucy. Increasing her socialization with the outside world via daily walks taught Lucy to be less reliant on Linda as her sole source of stimulation. Linda found that building Lucy's self-esteem was not difficult. She began to teach Lucy "sit," "down," and "stay." With these few words, they were able to communicate on a level that had previously been impossible. Linda commanded Lucy to "sit" and "stay" for each meal, thereby enlisting her dog as a worker, not a caretaker, and, most important, Linda attempted to shield Lucy from any inappropriate or self-destructive behavior on her owner's part. Armed with the knowledge that her self-destructive behavior was destructive to all around her, Linda was able to free Lucy from a life of "do as I do" and allow her to be the pet Linda had wanted in the first place.

Bend Me, Shape Me . . .

While it is perfectly natural that we sometimes need our dogs, and obvious that animals do have therapeutic value, it is nevertheless crucial that we recognize the difference between a working dog and a dog who is starved for work. A working dog has been trained or conditioned to respond to signals and commands as part of his daily routine, thereby making him useful to his human companions (i.e., seeing-eye dogs, therapy dogs, herding dogs, retrieving dogs, etc.). In fact, any dog who is simply required to follow basic commands from its people is a "working" dog. But the dog who has had little training (therefore little communications skills) and whose life is empty of necessary stimulation will search for ways to be useful, thereby taking jobs that they are not at all qualified for—witness Joan's dog, Topper; Michael's dog, Jake; Linda's dog, Lucy.

Because we have come to rely so heavily on the companionship of, rather than the working relationship with, our dogs, dogs are increasingly vulnerable to the neurotic behavior of their people. If we allow it to continue, it is likely to get worse. Because science has already taught us that stress ultimately takes its toll on the human body, wouldn't it then stand to reason that the same stress, once adopted by our dogs, will begin to take its toll on their bodies as well? Dogs are our best friends; surely we can treat them better than that!

Postscript: A funny thing happened while I was writing this chapter. My husband agreed to take my two young daughters out for an extended day so that I could have some "quiet" time to write. Without anything set in stone, I knew only that they would be back well after the dinner hour. As I am normally the primary caretaker of my children, I had been looking forward to the day with mixed emotions.

Nonetheless, when zero hour approached, the dogs and I kissed them all good-bye and I set out to complete my task.

The first couple of hours were as productive as I had planned but, as the day went on, I became preoccupied with the sounds outside the house, nervously hoping that each approaching car might be my family arriving home. I was clearly feeling uneasy about not being "in control" of and physically close to my children.

As I paced the floors, took the dogs for a long walk, and raided the fridge for just one more cookie, I realized that it was now early evening and I hadn't written more than four pages of acceptable copy. The stress of not having my family around was preoccupying my every thought.

I heard my golden retriever sigh (with extreme boredom), as he often does, and looked over to find him looking back at me with his head cocked to one side. As I, the all-knowing alpha of his pack, stared back into the black pools of never-ending information that are my dog's eyes, I realized that I was smack in the middle of a helplessly overwhelming attack of separation anxiety! For a fleeting moment I felt frighteningly like a Labrador retriever named Jake. Go figure . . .

Chapter 4

Who's Training Whom?

When the Dog Has the Upper Hand

Recently, I saw a man go up to a chiropractor at a cocktail party and ask for an adjustment. So, when I was approached by a woman at a recent fund-raising event who asked for some "dog-training advice," I was only too happy to help and even happier that I am not a dentist.

"**M**y dog Paisley** does the cutest thing just before I feed her. She goes into the kitchen, picks up her food bowl, finds me wherever I am in the house, and drops the bowl at my feet. Is she just hungry, or is she trying to tell me something?"

After listening to her story, I questioned the woman about her response to the dog dropping her bowl at her feet. She replied that she immediately took the bowl back to the kitchen and fed the dog. My answer to her two-part question was, "Yes, the dog probably was, in fact, hungry," and "Yes, she is clearly trying (in her own adorable way) to tell you something. That something is: 'Stop whatever you are doing and feed me!' " As the look of total confusion began to fade from her expression, I explained. "Your dog has trained you well. You see," I told her, "it has been said that 'the best dog trainers on earth are dogs.' "

One of the easiest traps to fall into when living with a dog is confusing who is training whom. In fact, in almost every human/dog relationship some element of reciprocal training exists. It's simply power playing, and to some dogs it is a harmless, intermittent game. However, there are dogs for whom this power struggle is the foundation of their very existence.

Dogs, like human children, need boundaries. Boundaries represent guidelines as to how far one can "push the envelope" but also give a clear picture of who is in charge. The necessity for limits is so great that if a dog's human caretaker does not create these boundaries, the dog will. However, when a dog creates the boundaries, they inadvertently become guidelines for us to follow, not the dog. In more households than we would like to admit, the dog is definitely running the show. Not your household, you say. Well maybe not but, just for fun, take a closer look.

When your dog brings you a toy and he wants to play, do you play? When he comes over to you and nuzzles his nose under your hand for a soothing scratch on the head, do you scratch? If he barks at you while you are relaxing, do you then turn and pay attention to the dog, thus asking him, "What do you want?" Do you, in response to his barking, toss him a treat, or even take him out for a walk? If the answer to even a few of these questions is yes, the fact is that your precious pup is definitely pushing you around. Be careful or you might soon be sleeping on the floor while your dog is spread out comfortably on your bed.

In each chapter so far, I have discussed the pack and what its power structure represents to a dog. In some form or another, a dog's behavior problems can almost always be traced to some confusion or misdirection pertaining to this "all-important" order. So, as in previous chapters, in this chapter and all chapters to follow, at some point, the dynamics of the pack must be examined. In this chapter we're going to need a theme song. It is "Leader of the Pack," and I want you to hum it every time your dog brings you his food dish, barks at you, brings you a toy to play with, or does just about any adorable thing that you have not yet commanded him to do.

Whether you know it or not, you are supposed to be the pack leader—alpha, top dog; quarterback, etc. If, however, you are not absolutely comfortable "holding the ball," the dog immediately picks up on that and identifies it as a weakness. Since nobody wants to be on a losing team (least of all a dog), and somebody has to call the plays, the dog instinctively takes the proverbial ball and runs with it. If you are not telling your dog what to do, your dog will be telling you what to do. And, if that's the case, be prepared to work like a dog.

Sometimes even the slightest inconsistency in your behavior is all it takes to "lose the ball." Take the lady at the party who asked me about her dog, Paisley: One day, during the normal mealtime routine, Paisley probably nudged her bowl before the woman picked it up. Thinking this gesture was "cute," she probably expressed delight, then fed the dog. Paisley immediately picked up on how this "trick" inspired the woman to fill her food bowl. As a result, whenever Paisley wanted to be fed, she simply performed her trick. The sticky part in all of this was that the dog no longer waited to be fed; instead, she simply used this trick to indicate that she wished to be fed. Not for a moment did the dog perceive picking up the bowl as a trick but, instead, as a direct command. Paisley's owner wasn't even aware that she was in the middle of a coup.

During the course of a normal, daily routine a dog learns to rely on signals as markers or indicators for behavior—regardless of who gives the signal. Actions that precede these signals can cause something to happen; for example, you pick up the dog's leash and the dog knows you are going to take him out for a walk. Similarly, actions that follow these signals can also cause something to happen (i.e., the dog touches the leash and you take him for a walk). For the dog, these actions or signals become powerful tools in controlling behavior. The question an effective owner needs to consider is whether it's his own behavior or his dog's that is being controlled.

In most relationships, whether professional or personal, establishing limits means establishing a comfort level, or a boundary line. Without discernible limits, however, someone always runs the risk of crossing that line. Not knowing where you stand in a relationship means that you must always be on the lookout for clues that let you know how to behave in a given situation. If your relationship with your dog is without discernible limits (i.e., sometimes you give him a tidbit of food from the table, sometimes you don't), then the dog is forced to constantly wait and watch for signs indicating whether he should take direction or give it; to follow this example through, he will watch to see if you are preparing to give him a table scrap or whether he has to jump to his feet and beg for the food. In the latter case, finding a comfort level becomes nearly impossible and the dog is almost always stressed.

When a dog is in charge, keeping track of you becomes his life's work. After all, if you are not in plain sight, how can he tell you what he wants? By the same token, letting you actually leave the house becomes downright hair-raising. If you are not there, how is the dog supposed to communicate his needs? Relaxation and rest for this dog are rarely an option.

Not surprisingly, it is often the same dogs who suffer from the effects of who's training whom and those who suffer from separation anxiety. The dog who suffers from separation anxiety cannot cope without you there to care for him, and the dog who suffers from who's training whom cannot cope without you there to tell you what to do. The behavioral results of these two conditions are very much the same. Without proper direction when you are around, dogs cannot develop healthy routines upon which to rely whether you are around or not. Because separation anxiety is becoming so prevalent in so many of our modern dogs, we often assume that leaving the dog must be the problem and separation anxiety the result. Because we feel guilty about leaving the dog alone all day, the issue of who's training whom is too often overlooked as the actual cause of a dog's behavioral problems. Additionally, our guilt has become the catalyst for our indulging the dog when we are finally together.

Good Night Little Doggy,
Good Night . . .

It had been almost three years since Annie and Chris had had an uninterrupted night's sleep. Their children, two and four years old respectively, had put them through all the normal parenting nighttime
traumas. Notwithstanding the 2:00 A.M. feedings, diaper changes, and
various "monsters" under the bed, they had finally taught both children
to sleep through the night. The dog, however, who was having her own
nighttime traumas, was proving to be a horse of a different color.

Kelly is an eight-year-old Shetland sheepdog who, until the time
she was four years old, was a dog owner's dream. She was obedience-
trained at an early age and had, until recently, been a full-time working
member of this family/pack. Annie, a jogger, took Kelly out each morning for a two-mile run. On the days when Annie and Chris came home
early enough from work, they would take the dog to a local park for addi-
tional exercise. Kelly never seemed to mind being home alone during
the day, and both Chris and Annie found it easy to keep up the dog's
"training" as part of their daily routine. It wasn't until almost a full year
after their first child was born that they noticed a change in their dog's
behavior.

It seemed, to the best of their sleep-deprived recollection, that at
least twice each night (between the hours of 2:00 and 5:00 A.M.) they
were awakened by the dog crying at the foot of their bed. The crying continued until either Chris or Annie would take Kelly into the kitchen and
give her a biscuit. This, and only this, seemed to calm the dog's whining.
But, shortly after they fell back asleep, the whining started all over again.

By the time the sun came up, the dog no longer seemed hungry and
rarely ate her breakfast. The food was left down for the remainder of the
day, so that Kelly was free to pick at it. When they refilled her bowl at
dinnertime, the dog didn't eat that meal either. So, at around 2:00 A.M.,
when the whining usually started, Chris and Annie just assumed that the
dog, who had picked at the morning meal and not eaten the evening
meal, must be hungry. Not wanting to begin the ritual of feeding the dog

a full meal in the middle of the night, they hoped the biscuits would satisfy the dog's hunger and they agreed that it was the easiest way to quiet
her during the night.

When the problem became unbearable for Annie and Chris, already
exhausted, they decided to lock the dog outside their bedroom, hoping
that the closed door between them would force Kelly to stop whining.
The whining, of course, continued and, in fact, became so loud that the
noise was beginning to wake the children. This was the last straw. But
until Chris and Annie could find help, they simply let Kelly back into
their bedroom and resumed the frustrating nighttime routine. At least
this way, they reasoned, she would wake only them and not the children.
Their desperate search for a solution led them to me.

Kelly was, as Chris had described her during our first phone conversation, an adorable, energetic, canine clown. She was not only attentive to the children but also acutely aware of Chris and Annie's every
move. They were eager to show off some of the training they had previously done with Kelly, and I was pleased to see that this very smart little
dog was just as eager to follow their commands. She would not, however,
work (follow commands) for free. The couple explained that the dog
would obey a command only for a food reward.

As our conversation focused on the time frame of the dog's behavior
change, Chris observed that the trouble had started about the time their
eldest child had turned one year old. Chris had always done the night
feedings and he fondly remembered the dog dutifully sharing the
responsibilities of the "night shift." He recalled the dog sitting diligently beside him each evening, staring lovingly at both father and son.
Chris was so proud of his dog's loyal nature during those long nights that
he felt obliged to reward Kelly with a biscuit as soon as he had finished
feeding the baby.

This routine—the one between man and dog—continued (Chris was
embarrassed to admit) well after the baby required a night feeding.
Since he was no longer getting up to warm a bottle and feed the baby, he
kept a bowl of treats on his nightstand "just in case." Having the biscuits
at arms' length meant that he wouldn't have to go all the way into the
kitchen to get the dog a treat. Whenever the dog nudged his hand, he

would simply toss the dog a treat. But gradually "just in case" had turned into two or three times a night for the past three years.

In recounting the nighttime routine of the last three years, Chris recalled going back to the same routine after their second son had been born two years later. Chris would feed the baby, then take the dog into the kitchen for a biscuit. He then admitted to doing something that, until now, not even his wife was aware of. Whenever there was breast milk left in the baby's bottle after a feeding, Chris would pour it into the dog's water dish. Annie's jaw practically hit the floor as he described what he thought was a harmless gesture, the result of his not wanting to waste the milk. That was, Chris admitted after reflecting a bit more, around the time the dog stopped eating her dog food altogether.

The culprit had reared its ugly head! Actually, it had been there all along, quietly hiding behind Chris's need to emotionalize his relationship with his dog. This need, however, had created a very specific set of behavioral signals for the dog (and later the man) to follow. While Chris was simply feeding the baby and then rewarding the dog, the dog was learning to rely on the feedings as a signal that preceded a reward. After the nighttime feedings were no longer necessary for the baby, they were still, in fact, quite necessary for the dog.

When the signals (i.e., Chris getting the bottle and feeding the baby) were no longer a part of the nighttime routine, the dog—not understanding why the routine had suddenly changed—began to nudge the man's hand, prompting the food reward. When the nudging no longer worked, the dog began to whine, part in protest and part in distress. The whining then became the signal that prompted Chris to reward the dog and, voilà, the dog was now successfully signaling the man to produce the reward.

What had begun as the man sharing a tender moment with his dog had become a classic case of the dog training the man. And to make matters worse, now the dog (who clearly preferred treats and breast milk to dog food) would not eat even a speck of her own food. Chris looked over at his wife, who was still shocked at having learned that her dog had been sharing her baby's breast milk, and admitted to feeling a bit like Dr. Frankenstein.

Now that we were all in agreement as to how the monster had been created, the plan was simply to disassemble the monster. The first and most important step was to stop taking direction from the dog. This meant that any annoying (or attention-seeking) behavior on the dog's part had to be completely ignored. Next, food was to be given only as a reward for the dog taking direction from Chris or Annie, not the other way around. Because feeding a dog is a ritual that should not be taken lightly, I explained that Kelly must be required to work for her meals. Chris was to be in charge of the morning meal and Annie in charge of the evening meal. They were to call the dog into the kitchen ("come"), fill the food dish, and tell the dog to "sit." If she obeyed, whoever was doing the feeding was to verbally praise the dog and then tell her to "stay." The food was then to be put on the ground and the dog, after a few seconds, released and told she could now eat ("okay"). After fifteen minutes, whether the dog ate the food or not, the bowl was to be lifted off the floor. The same routine was to be repeated for the evening meal. The dog might skip as many as a few days' worth of meals, but it wasn't likely. When a dog is hungry, and eventually he will be, he will eat . . . even dog food!

Next, we needed to stop the whining in the middle of the night. I suggested that the couple begin this part of the retraining on a weekend because any lost sleep could be made up in the form of a nap during the day. At bedtime, they were to tell the dog to "go to your place," which was a dog bed in the corner of their bedroom. That was the last thing I wanted them to say to her before getting into their own bed and going to sleep. No matter how often or loudly the dog whined, they were to ignore her. No matter what she tried to do to get their attention, they were still to ignore her.

I assured them that when modifying this kind of learned or habitual behavior in a dog, it shouldn't take more than two or three nights before they saw a change. After exhausting all efforts to get Chris and Annie to obey her commands—to no avail—she would eventually just give up. Annie and Chris seemed relieved at seeing a light at the end of this tunnel.

I cautioned them as to the importance of being committed to this plan. Once the exercise had begun, there was no turning back. If they started and then eventually gave in, the dog would only learn to perseverate and would become even more of a problem.

The daytime routine was just as important and equally as rigorous. Giving, not taking, direction from this dog was crucial. Since all dogs are looking for direction from their human caretakers, Chris and Annie should not feel any guilt in telling their dog what they expect her to do. Since dogs are a "working" species by nature, giving this dog a job should not only be easy but fun.

I suggested a simple, five-minute lesson in basic obedience. This was to be done each day as often as their schedules allowed. Treats were not to be used during these sessions, only voice reward, as this dog already knew the meaning of the words. Follow-through was also key to the success of this exercise. If the dog did not obey (because she was used to working for a treat), Chris or Annie were to physically—and gently—help Kelly successfully complete the command. The only time this dog was to receive food as a reward was when she was being fed a meal.

With two children and two full-time careers, Chris and Annie had little downtime of their own, and Kelly's physical exercise routine had naturally fallen off considerably. After explaining the paramount importance and direct connection of exercise to behavior in dogs, Annie agreed to enlist the help of a neighbor to take Kelly for two long walks each day.

As I had suspected (and prayed) would happen, Kelly stopped whining after two full nights of being totally ignored by her "parents." She now works for her meals and, because she no longer receives food at any other time of day, she is actually hungry enough to eat both breakfast and dinner. The daily walks have tired her out considerably. So much, in fact, that, by the time Chris and Annie have the boys ready for bed, it seems that the dog is ready as well.

All in all, after implementing the new "regime" into their daily routine, things were pretty much back to normal for the whole family. I spoke to Chris and Annie several months later, just before Annie was to give birth to their third child. Chris assured me (and Annie) that during this 2:00 A.M. feeding shift, he would be much more careful to feed only the baby and not the dog.

. . .

Dogs actually require very little of their human companions when you consider the devotion and undying love they give in return. A scratch on the head and two square meals a day can be a hefty reward for a job well done. But keeping an eye on who's doing the job and who's getting the reward is an art unto itself. As a responsible modern dog owner, you must be sharper than the dog. No legitimate boss would pay a worker for a job that he was doing himself; the same holds true here.

Coming to terms with the fact that good parenting requires discipline based on boundaries is the first step in raising a healthy, well-behaved dog (or a child, for that matter). Dogs rely on us to remind them when they are bending or forgetting the rules. If, at closer glance, you are beginning to feel as if your dog is calling the shots, changing the balance of the scales—the enforcement of the rules—does not have to be terribly difficult at all. And, if it doesn't help, you can always go back to working for the dog.

Another problem born of "who's training whom" confusion that clearly warrants a closer look as it grows more common is "reaction" behavior. It is Dr. Nicholas Dodman, author of *Dogs Behaving Badly*, who has accurately defined this behavior as "reactive." Reactive, in this case, means a specific behavior that is triggered by a certain stimulus.

We have all known at least one dog suffering from reactive behavior. They balk on the street for what seems like no apparent reason; they fly into an uncontrollable, inconsolable frenzy when the doorbell rings; they stuff anything that's not nailed down into their mouths whenever a visitor comes to call (my golden retriever does this). The list goes on and on and, more often than not, these antics demand immediate attention lest the behavior escalate beyond any tolerable level. These dogs closely resemble the dogs in chapter 3, "My Dog/Myself." They are the dogs whose behavior is often a direct result, or even an imitation, of their owner's.

As I've already discussed, dogs are hypersensitive to our signals, and the genetic predisposition of certain breeds guides them to certain behaviors (such as herding or retrieving). Combining these two facts, it makes sense that a dog's genetically predisposed behavior could then be magnified, or lessened (as the case may be), depending on his owner's reaction to that behavior.

If this is so, as I believe it is, then those little balkers and barkers might be putting on a show just to get a rise out of us. Who do they think they are? Well, the real question is: Who have we been teaching them to be?

Reactions Speak Louder Than Words . . .

"Come on, Dillon, come on, baby, please, Dillon, please . . ." The woman—a tall, athletic, well-dressed, seemingly normal and consenting adult—was down on one knee, begging her dog to move forward along the street. The dog, a sweet-faced West Highland terrier, sat, steadfastly connected to the sidewalk, staring blankly back at the woman. As she begged, the dog seemed less concerned about what he should do but, instead, fixated on what the woman was going to do next. A moment later, the woman heaved a sigh of defeat, picked the dog up, petted him apologetically, and walked home.

What was different about this day that was different from any other? Nothing. This was the usual morning routine for Polly and her dog, Dillon. Polly would take Dillon for a walk, and Dillon (after eliminating almost immediately) would walk thirty or so feet and then stop and sit, with absolutely no intention of moving anywhere, anytime, in the foreseeable future. Polly—thinking something must be wrong with her dog—panicked. "Dillon, are you okay?" she would ask in an alarmed tone. After about five seconds of pleading, Polly then scooped up her dog and brought him back into the house, petting and comforting him all the way. After several months of repeating this pattern, walk after walk, Dillon eventually refused to walk at all.

I first met Polly at a group obedience class. I was not the instructor, but, in fact, one of the students. My golden retriever, Blue, was five months old at the time and very ready, as all young dogs are, for some group training. We struck up a conversation after class and I offered her some tips of my own.

I explained to Polly that dogs often stop short on the street. Whether because the dog simply needs to get its bearings, or only needs a moment's rest, many dogs, like Dillon, sometimes just stop dead in their tracks during a walk. Another term for this is "balking" and, if doing so prompts a dramatic response—either negative or positive—from another pack member, the chances are that the dog will start to repeat the behavior to elicit the response. Such was definitely the case with Polly and Dillon.

Because Dillon was a terrier, his personality might already have been of a stubborn slant. His standoff on the sidewalk with Polly might simply have been of the "I'm going this way, you're going that way" variety. If Polly had waited out this willful display, it might have been over as quickly as it started. But Polly's response to Dillon's complaint sent a dangerous message of weakness to this dog, and quickly convinced him that he must be in charge. And, to make matters worse, by responding so dramatically and immediately to her dog's refusal to walk, Polly actually initiated a pattern that would eventually teach her dog not to walk at all.

The strong feelings we have for our dogs can (and do) often cloud our rational judgment when trying to solve our canine behavioral dilemmas. It is, however, this rational (or irrational, as the case may be) judgment that provides the signals the dog relies on as boundaries for its own behavior. Recognizing the difference between willful disobedience and learned disobedience, and being careful not to foster either, requires little more than the ability to disconnect yourself from your dog emotionally—even for a moment. Easier said than done, true, but not if you know that doing so will help your dog overcome behavior that is clearly undermining his entire well-being. Because Dillon refused to walk, he got very little physical exercise. His sedentary lifestyle encouraged two other predisposed terrier traits—digging and barking. These activities kept him busy while Polly was away each day at work. Gradually, Dillon and Polly's relationship seemed to have far more problems than pleasure.

I thought Polly should begin by tackling Dillon's "walking" problem. Doing so would enable her to give her dog the exercise he so desperately needed, which might result in the diminishment of the other problems. Getting into a sidewalk tug-of-war with the dog was not the answer. Instead, I thought Polly need only raise Dillon's collar a bit higher around his neck (picture what the lead looks like on a dog prancing around a show ring) and simply walk.

Walking a dog can be a bit like riding a horse. If you concentrate on where you are—rather than where you are going—the horse is likely to trip or, at the very least, become confused about where you both are headed. But, if you look beyond (to where you are going), with heels down and a bit of confidence surging through the reins, both horse and rider move gracefully forward as a team. Walking a dog requires a similar team spirit. Dogs sense when a person is not certain where he or she is headed. This, like the horse and rider, can knock the whole equation off balance—usually leaving at least one of you flat on your ass.

So, first Polly needed to resolve that she, at least, was willing to give new meaning to the phrase "walking the dog." First, I showed Polly that it could be done by my taking Dillon for a walk. After all, Dillon didn't know me and was far less likely to put on the brakes with a stranger. Polly was shocked by the dog's steady step forward. He stopped once to eliminate but, once finished, kept up the pace. About halfway across our third block (which was farther than this dog had walked in months), I gave Polly the leash. I coached her to not leave too much slack in the lead lest Dillon think he was once again steering himself.

Polly smiled for the remainder of our walk, which was considerably longer than she had ever hoped to go on her first try. Dillon seemed to be smiling, too—almost as if he found confidence in the new way Polly was walking him. That night she called to report that Dillon was so exhausted from their walk that, rather than following her from room to room as usual, he was now fast asleep in his bed.

The following week we met again at obedience class and Polly exclaimed that their walks were miraculously changed. Dillon stopped now only when Polly allowed him to. Remembering to be careful not to react at all to Dillon's undesirable balking, Polly boasted that she now simply kept walking, and, to her delight, so did her dog.

Salty Dog

Solving one problem often results in the solving of many. Thankfully, such was the case with Dillon's digging and barking. However, what can begin as the solution to one problem sometimes, unfortunately, becomes the source of another.

Appreciating a dog's keen attention to signals is always a great tool when solving behavior problems. Getting into the dog's mind and trying to see the world from his perspective tends to change the view entirely. One does not have to be an animal behaviorist or a professional trainer to master this technique. Simply practice role-playing by imagining that you are the dog and the dog is you. This, and a bit of good detective work, will almost always lead you to the answer. Such was the case with a very astute Portuguese water dog named Salty.

Salty had more problems than you could shake a stick at. To begin with, he suffered terribly from separation anxiety. His owners, Jill and Michael, worked from nine to five. This left Salty with far too much time alone and far too little to occupy his time. The dog was, predictably, destructive. First he destroyed his owners' property, and eventually he began to harm himself.

Salty seemed determined to run away. He sometimes jumped the chain-link fence, or dug his way out of the yard, but no matter what his methods, he clearly wished to find more interesting ways to spend his days. Unfortunately, he had been caught by local animal control one too many times and the couple was running out of options—after all, they had to go to work. Jill and Michael ultimately decided to install an electric fence and hoped it would work. It worked, but what should have been the end of the problem was just the beginning of another.

Recently, Salty had developed a new habit. He would enthusiastically greet any guest who came to visit but then go positively ballistic when they tried to leave. If anyone even attempted to put on their coat or head in the direction of the front door, Salty started barking wildly and fiercely snapping at the escapee. Needless to say, this behavior was not only driving Salty's owners nuts, it was also driving their friends away. Because Jill and Michael were neighbors of mine and I had heard Salty's "concert" once or twice from my own yard, I wasn't surprised when they called to ask for help. I grabbed my "bag of tricks" and headed over to see what I could do. I informed my husband that I would be home in about two hours—provided Salty let me out of the house.

After explaining the details of Salty's daily excursions and their ultimate decision to install the electric fence, Jill and Michael also described how the dog sometimes spent hours digging at one spot (inside, by the front door), trying to get out of the house. At first Jill was adamantly against installing the electric fence but finally, feeling she had little choice, she gave in. Salty needed to be outside when they were not at home or he might just destroy the house altogether. Also, she explained, "The fence really does work. He hasn't even tried to leave the property since we had it put in."

I explained that Portuguese water dogs are in the "working" group of dog breeds and, along with needing an enormous amount of daily exercise, take their job within their pack very seriously. Keeping things (in this case, the family) together was part of their natural behavior—thus, a significant reason for Salty's separation anxiety. If the pack went in separate directions, the dog was painfully unable to exercise his indigenous need to keep them all together—all factors that encouraged Salty's daily escapes in the hope of finding his family. But, other than the routine advice about building this dog's self-esteem through obedience training, and giving him a good deal more exercise each day, I could find no obvious reason for Salty's attempts at taking hostages whenever Jill and Michael had company, so about this I could offer no advice.

We talked more about the importance of employing the dog as a working member of the pack and socializing him to the outside world so that he would feel less panicked about Jill and Michael leaving him each day, but I honestly felt I was reaching. There was clearly a separate reason for Salty's outbursts and I wondered if I had simply missed it. After giving the couple the best advice I could offer and reminding them to watch for signs that preceded Salty's outbursts, I got up to leave.

The moment I stood up, the most fascinating thing happened. Salty began to whine. This, interesting though it might have been, was not what intrigued me. I was deliberately indifferent to his whining and waited to see what would come next. As I began to put my coat on, Salty's whining escalated to hysterical barking (the kind that Jill and Michael had described). Rather than aggressive ("You can't leave"), Salty's barking was of the "Please don't go" variety. It was this distinction that intrigued me. Within seconds, Salty was hysterical, salivating and nipping at my feet. Like any good dog trainer/self-proclaimed behaviorist,

I stood by and watched—smiling, of course. I was smiling not because I enjoyed watching poor Salty come unhinged, but rather because I believed I had found the precious missing piece to the puzzle. If I was correct, this piece would explain Salty's outrageous lapse in manners whenever anyone tried to leave the house. I quickly sat back down, which I suspected would calm the dog—and it did. Jill released her grip on his collar and we all gradually regained our composure. I inquired as to the connection between this behavior and the installation of the electric fence. Michael thought for a moment and then almost shouted, "Oh my god, he began doing this about three or four weeks after we put in the electric fence!"

It was now clear to me (and fast becoming clear to Jill and Michael) that their dog's behavior was reactive. Some dogs are prone to reactive behavior by the nature of their genetic map, but all dogs can be taught reactive behavior. I believed Salty's actions were due to factors both inherent and learned.

First, Salty's keen instincts kept sharp his awareness of each person's location whenever Salty was in a group. Second, his learned response to the "zap" that was now delivered each time he neared the boundaries of his yard made him protective of anyone else headed toward those boundaries.

I explained to Michael and Jill what I believed was the cause of Salty's problem. Whenever someone was going out of the house, Salty was clearly stressed about the dangers the outdoors now posed—given the invisible electric current surrounding the yard. The whining was, I believed, Salty's way of releasing some of that stress. A first warning, so to speak. If that warning went unheeded, and it always did because visitors were not aware of the electric fence at all, Salty (being the fine working dog that he was) did whatever was necessary to keep them safe. Thus, the reason for the lapse in poise, kind of a DANGER! DANGER! cry. So, whenever someone tried to leave the house, he was not trying to attack at all but, in fact, to protect.

Now I knew I could help. The first order of business was to convince this dog that the invisible monster outside was not a monster at all. The best thing for Jill and Michael to do was not to let someone out of their house but, instead, to take them out—with the dog. Getting Salty ready first would be the most prudent way to handle this exercise. Just before the end of any visit, Jill called Salty to "come" and snapped on his leash. Then she told him to "sit" and "wait." Then, everyone else could get ready to leave. I advised Jill that, at this point, I thought it best that she took Salty outside and waited there for everyone to come out to them. This way the dog could see that anyone who came outside was still safe. It was also a good idea to command Salty to "sit" again once outside. This would relax him a bit more and, again, he could witness the remainder of the "exodus" without incident. The "brush up" on basic obedience would serve to remind Salty that he was a pack member and not a pack leader.

Because the electric fence had caused such a sensitive and severe reaction in this dog, I thought it best that they turn it off, at least for a while. Trying it again at another time might prove just as detrimental, but desensitizing the dog first might make him less reactive at some later date.

As for the separation anxiety, I thought Jill and Michael should work on that as a completely separate issue (see chapter 3, "My Dog/Myself"), with further training and exercise as we had discussed earlier. On the whole, sending stronger leadership signals would help Jill and Michael to convince Salty to leave the entertaining to them. I am relieved to say that, for the most part, Salty is no longer worried that anyone venturing outside the confines of his "den" will be zapped by the "invisible monster." He, like all good hosts, has taken to walking his guests outside and watching as they leave his "territory," making sure that all is well. Lesson learned: Don't ever underestimate the power of a dog's mind.

Whether instinctive or reactive, your dog's behavior is ultimately your responsibility. Being careful to send clear "leadership" messages to your dog is not cruel—on the contrary, it's imperative to the animal's well-being. Dogs—all dogs—want a clear picture of where they rank in the group with whom they live. This knowledge keeps them focused on their life-sustaining job: that of pleasing their owners. Without a definitive place in the pack, the dog has no sense of his own purpose in his world. Any dog in this position will surely not fare well.

The most fascinating part of spending one's life observing animal behavior is discovering and rediscovering just how extraordinary dogs can be. If we were to learn only one thing from our dogs, it should be to heed their behavior as a barometer for what is right and not right with their world.

No one can or should ever tell you how to love your dog. But sound advice about how your dog needs to live in order to remain psychologically healthy is worth heeding. As I peruse the many pet specialty stores that have popped up on almost every street corner in just about every urban and suburban landscape, I am baffled by the selection of "doggy entertainment" available in the marketplace. Have we become so misguided that we have lost sight of the fact that the dog's greatest form of entertainment is to entertain us? I think we have. We need to remember that what the dog needs is a legitimate job. We should, at the very least, realize that a toy currently on the market—one that delivers treats to the dog while you are not at home—is not going to teach your dog who's in charge. We should also keep in mind how hugely important it is that we put the dog to work when we get home.

So, for all the budding alphas out there trying to be the perfect dog "parents," remember to keep humming "Leader of the Pack" and, above all, to keep a sharp eye on who's training whom or, before long, it might be you heading into the obedience ring.

Chapter 5

Rover Rage

Why Dogs Are Nasty

*With road rage now a legally recognized offense and dri-
vers assaulting each other on highways for such minor
infractions as tailgating, is it really all that surprising
that our dogs are forgetting their manners as well?*

With the pitbull all but replacing the semiautomatic weapon, a
well-adjusted dog sometimes seems as hard to find as a retired Beanie
Baby. With more than 4.5 million dog bites reported each year (and
imagine how many aren't reported), the odds are greater that you'll be
bitten by a dog than that you will stay happily married. Of course, there's

nothing funny about a dog bite (especially if you've ever been bitten—and I have been), but this is as good a time as any to take a long look at why dogs bite.

Dogs bite, for one, because they are dogs. When a dog is trying to send a message of stress or discomfort, and that message is not clearly received, the bite then becomes the messenger. The message may be one of fear, anger, territoriality, unfamiliarity, or just plain nastiness, but the key to eliminating the message is to understand it.

Since the earliest man/dog partnerships, man has respected dog's self-preserving right to defend itself. In fact, the dog's natural protective nature was often considered desirable when contemplating the addition of a dog to one's family. If an intruder crossed a territorial boundary, the dog would be there to respond accordingly, and afterward would be rewarded for its good work and loyalty. Stories of dogs protecting their humans and their territory have for centuries been traded with great pride. Well before the invention of home security alarms, the dog was man's steady, reliable protector. Boundaries may have been drawn up by deeds, but they were protected and enforced by dogs.

With contemporary cities and suburbs overflowing with dogs, and property lines ending inches from the thresholds of our front doors, it's hardly surprising that dogs sometimes have a hard time discerning whose territory is whose. With relationships and living arrangements changing sometimes as often as biannually, the confusion of whom and what to protect has become the almost constant dilemma of the modern dog.

Having spent the majority of the day waiting inside the fortress of the walls we call home, once permitted outside the dog is overloaded with strange smells, strange sounds, and even stranger faces. The dog's need to eliminate, coupled with its need to claim some small piece of real estate in the public jungle (and to a dog there is nothing public about space), is controlled by the length of a leash. Sticking close to their "charge," diligently on guard to protect the one constant that is truly theirs (that would be you), the result is an otherwise well-mannered canine who becomes dangerously sensitive about sharing its space, not to mention its people. This behavior is one of the hallmarks of the latchkey dog.

For years, my work training dogs had been concerned mainly with the usual routine of puppy training and basic problem-solving. Until recently, I was confronted with only the occasional "monster mongrel." Having done most of my work inside a large city, I attributed the lack of aggressive "city dogs" to the fact that, given their densely populated surroundings, they must all be well socialized. I had even come to the uneducated conclusion that living in a city was far better for a dog than living in a suburban area.

If you lived in a metropolis, you had little choice but to interact with your dog. Sending your dog out the back door and forgetting about him simply wasn't an option. When you arrived home (after a long day apart from the dog), you and your dog would spend the remainder of your waking hours reaffirming the bonds of the pack. All activities—eating, walking, playing, socializing, and sleeping—were a joint effort.

During the last few years, however, I have been called upon to assist a dramatically increasing number of people with trigger-happy dogs— dogs who snarl or snap at anyone (including their owners) who threatens to invade their space. As the success of much of what I do rests on properly determining why a dog behaves the way it does in a given situation, I theorized that there must be some common thread linking the living patterns of these dogs who demonstrated such similar symptoms. Once this common thread was determined, the source of, and therefore solution to, the problem would hopefully be close at hand. After compiling as much data as was necessary to map out the similarities between all of these dogs, I was surprised to realize that what conditions I had once assumed were good for the dog were, in fact, the very source of these dogs' increasingly undesirable behavior.

Dogs are naturally social creatures. Their very survival depends upon their understanding of the complex relations with their pack. It is the interplay between these relationships and the pack's living environment that determine how a dog will behave in a specific situation. For instance, take the single-owner dog. If this owner is fortunate enough to be able to bring the dog to work every day and the work environment is one where people are constantly walking in and out (such as a retail store), that owner's dog would undoubtedly be at ease with many people milling about. The sounds of the street—car horns honking, buses passing—become a nonthreatening, white noise. Because the dog's owner reacts with ease to the people and the noise, the dog is content to follow suit and passes the day in a relaxed state—allowing the people and noise to become part of its immediate environment.

But what if the owner wasn't so fortunate and the dog was forced to spend the day alone at home, waiting? The dog would then associate the outside sounds as threats to its immediate environment and, when its pack member (owner) finally returned to the "den," going outdoors—face-to-face with all of the intrusions—might literally be too much for the dog to handle. Entering a large group of people who are blowing horns—a sound once off in the distance—loudly in your face can be overwhelming, especially if you've spent most of your day alone. It's kind of like waking from a long sleep and finding yourself in a front-row seat at the Big Apple Circus! This is just one of the reasons why an otherwise good-natured dog might become a bit unpredictable when faced with the stress of full-blown sensory overload.

Dog size is another factor. Indeed, size is sometimes the sole reason that a person chooses a particular breed to live with. Being small gives some dogs the advantage (or in this case, disadvantage) of never having to go outside. Cleanup is not a large task, so allowing the dog to eliminate in the house makes life easy for the owner. Unfortunately, when a dog loses immediate contact with the outside world, his life becomes much harder. Never leaving the house turns the sounds outside into veritable monsters. A dog in this situation eventually becomes obsessively vocal, as if constantly sounding an alarm that danger is near. Such a dog is often very "snappy," as well, even to friendly visitors whom it perceives as intruders entering territory that belongs to only the dog and its pack. Small dogs have always been and will always be desirable for many, regardless of the square footage of living space. But, unbeknownst to many prospective owners, many of these smaller dogs (i.e., terriers) have been bred (for thousands of years) specifically to hunt and kill vermin. With a built-in predatory mechanism that involves seizing anything moving on the ground, hundreds of stepping feet on a city street, or in a busy schoolyard, may present too tempting a prospect. These dogs are literally rat-seeking missiles and, for any self-respecting terrier, capturing a moving foot would seem like a job well done.

Now, add to this equation the fact that this naturally energetic hunter has had little else to do all day but lie around and wait and you begin to get a sense of the problem.

Once thought to be inhumane, the incidence of city dwellers owning large dogs has increased a thousandfold. These dogs often need larger spaces to stretch their legs and release the natural energy that is stored while waiting around the house day after day. Without the opportunity to burn this "rocket fuel," undesirable behavior cannot help but rear its ugly head.

Socialization is probably the most important ingredient in raising the well-mannered dog. Regardless of a dog's size, if it is not properly exposed to the outside world from the tender young age of just twelve weeks, personality problems will manifest as this dog ages.

Dogs are naturally gregarious, social creatures that must be constantly included in the communal workings of their environment in order to remain companionable. Whether home is a fourth-floor walk-up or a ten-acre spread, even the sweetest golden retriever can become antisocial if left alone for the greater part of its days and not properly socialized during its nights. That said, going from "solitary confinement" to the "state fair" can be more than anyone could take. Unfortunately, many city, as well as suburban, latchkey dogs are doing it daily.

Clearly our need to go out into the world—often for many hours at a time—in order to earn a living does not mitigate our desire to share our lives with a dog. Staying at home with the dog is the ideal option, but if most of us did that we couldn't afford dog food. Perhaps some middle ground exists where both man and his dog could live with more mutual satisfaction, and with many fewer dog bites. I, for one, believe it does exist.

Pop, Crackle, Snap . . .

Bonnie and Clyde were waiting for me. They knew well before I reached to ring the doorbell that I had arrived. The traditional antecedents of a visit (elevator doors opening, footsteps in the hall) had given them warning. The pair was, as always, poised for battle. The door opened and

I stepped inside slowly and cautiously, as I had been warned to do and, to the amazement of those inside, without incident. For a moment Clyde and Bonnie's owners looked at me as if I possessed some kind of magical powers, having thus far escaped being attacked by at least one of their dogs.

I spent the first few moments speaking directly to the dogs, then knelt down to their level, letting them adjust to my unfamiliar appearance and scent. After about a minute of the usual noisy "war dance" around "the strange visitor," they lost interest. Then I slowly stood up and introduced myself to Katherine and Madeline, the human members of this pack. We moved into the living room, sat down (this time in chairs), and began to try to unravel the mystery of what had become Bonnie and Clyde's reign of terror with Katherine and Madeline's friends, scores of unsuspecting delivery people, and countless numbers of passersby in the street.

I began with my usual list of "getting-to-know-you" questions. Where and at what age were the dogs purchased and/or adopted? How much basic training ("sit," "come," "down," "stay," etc.) had the dogs been taught? How much of that basic training was used on a daily basis with the dogs? Where did the dogs sleep? What did the dogs eat? How much did they eat? Who fed the dogs? How quickly did they consume their food? How much daily exercise did the dogs get? How much daily exposure to the outside world did they receive? At what age did that daily exposure begin? Were the dogs allowed to eliminate indoors?

The facts began to assemble themselves. Bonnie and Clyde, both miniature wirehaired dachshunds, were littermates (brother and sister) and had been purchased from a reputable breeder in a fairly remote suburb of New Hampshire. Katherine and Madeline purchased Clyde when he was twelve weeks old. He was a gregarious fellow who loved people. So much so, in fact, that he was able to elicit affection from anyone and everyone he met. Albeit a bit vocal and high-strung (as dachshunds inherently can be), Clyde was, for the most part, a lovely—and loved—dog. Almost a year and a half later, Bonnie joined the household of Katherine, Madeline, and Clyde.

It seemed the breeder, who had intended to keep Bonnie for the purpose of "showing" her, called to say that she had decided the dog was just not "show quality"—something about her being too small and frail to breed. She thought Katherine and Madeline might be interested in a second dog. Practically speaking, they were not. Emotionally speaking, however, they hung up the phone, got in the car, and made the long journey from Manhattan to New Hampshire to pick up Bonnie. Here, it seems, is where their problems began.

Having spent her entire life surrounded by other dogs and the peaceful solitude of the New Hampshire countryside, Bonnie was wholly unprepared for the hustle and bustle of a big city. Because obedience training had not been part of her daily, past routine, Bonnie preferred communicating with Clyde rather than with Katherine and Madeline. She quickly became Clyde's mentor (alpha) and reminded him every chance she got of how a "real dog" was supposed to behave.

From the outset, Bonnie exhibited genuine fear when required to use the busy sidewalks as a toilet. Because she was quite small, Katherine and Madeline thought it acceptable for Bonnie to eliminate in the house on paper, thus making her visits to the "mean streets" less frequent. In contrast, Clyde continued to eliminate only outdoors. As Katherine and Madeline both had careers that necessitated long hours away from home, they found solace in knowing Bonnie and Clyde now had each other for company. As the months passed, taking walks with both dogs at once became difficult, as Clyde wanted to "meet and greet" and Bonnie was more inclined to "freeze-dance" her way around the sea of legs and feet that overwhelmed her whenever she left the house. (One country mouse was no match for Bonnie, but walking through hundreds of moving city feet gave "ratting" a whole new meaning.) Both women found the easiest way around the problem was to carry Bonnie and walk Clyde.

As the months passed, Bonnie began to randomly snap at a passing foot in the street whenever she was put down on the ground, a behavior that evolved into snapping at visitors whenever they tried to enter the apartment. To make matters even worse, Clyde was now beginning to notice and imitate Bonnie's behavior. "Once," Madeline explained, "the phone rang while I was sitting on the couch petting Clyde. I quickly got up to answer it and he snapped at me as I moved off the couch. Now, every time the phone rings, he jumps up from wherever he is and starts barking at and chasing after whoever is trying to answer the phone."

The women also owned a country house on several acres about two hours outside Manhattan. They spent most weekends there, and naturally the dogs would fill their days roaming freely, happily chasing the occasional field mouse and navigating the obstacle courses that the countryside presented. During these weekends Bonnie had no fear of the outdoors and seemed, on the whole, less nervous. It was as if the city was a place that she visited and the country was really "home." Of course, with work left behind in the city, Katherine and Madeline were able to spend a great deal more time at home, with the dogs. Country life seemed to suit them all. Unless, that is, a visitor came to call.

Even people who were not strangers to Bonnie and Clyde had to be on their guard at all times in the dogs' presence. Any sudden movements might ignite an explosion of noise and teeth. Madeline mentioned that the dogs might even get used to a visitor while downstairs in the main part of the house, but if the person went upstairs and came down again, the dogs would go after him as if he had just come into the house for the first time. The single saving grace in all of this seemed to be the size of the dogs. Because they were small and of no significant weight, most people were inclined to forgive what seemed like a "harmless snap" from a little dog. As grateful as Katherine and Madeline were for the forgiving nature of their dogs' victims, they knew something had to be done about these explosive episodes.

This brought us back to the answers to the initial set of questions that I put to Katherine and Madeline. The information they had given me up to this point was key in understanding why the dogs were behaving the way they were. Now I needed to know more specifically the dynamics of the dogs' relationships with Katherine and Madeline in order to help solve the problem.

According to Katherine and Madeline, the dogs were fed in the morning and the food was left down for the remainder of the day. When either Katherine or Madeline arrived home at night, they discarded whatever remained in the dogs' bowls from the morning meal and refilled their bowls with the evening meal. It seemed, anyway, that the dogs didn't really like to eat until both the women were home.

As for their preference of resting places, being "long-bodied" dogs, it was difficult for Bonnie and Clyde to jump to a surface high off the ground, so Katherine thought they would have better access to the furniture if foot stools were placed near the couches, chairs, and beds. So the answer to my question was that basically, wherever the dogs wanted to rest, they rested. Madeline did mention, however, that if one of the women was out of the house and one was inside the home, the dogs preferred lying by the front door rather than on the couch or the bed.

Katherine and Madeline explained that, fundamentally, they understood the importance of basic obedience and had therefore taught Clyde how to "sit," "stay," and "come." However, Clyde never really obeyed the "come" command; he seemed to "come" whenever he was ready. Bonnie was initially a willing student but, after a while, the daily practice of their commands seemed more like an interruption to the dogs than a way to communicate with them. "Besides," Katherine said, "they are so small, do they really need to be obedience trained?" That was the $64 million question!

Obedience training, I explained, was more a way of establishing a common language than anything else. It was through this language that a person could send a message to a dog that the dog could actually understand. The real underlying importance of the message, however, was not that the dog should "sit" or "lie down" or "come here" (even though that was often necessary). Rather, it was a way of letting the dog know that you were his caretaker, not the other way around. By failing to establish themselves as the pack's leaders, Katherine and Madeline left the job open for Bonnie and Clyde.

In addition, allowing a dog who is not required to follow instructions from a human to indiscriminately elevate himself to "higher ground," or jump on furniture at will, merely strengthens that dog's conviction that he is in charge. This is not to say that if you choose to spend your nights in bed with your dog or enjoy sharing your couch with your dog that it can't be done. Feel free to do so, but first make it clear to the dog that it is at your instruction that the dog be allowed on "higher ground." If the dog leaves the ground and leaps up on a piece of furniture, simply command the dog "off." Help, if necessary, and then praise. Then tell the dog to sit, and again, if necessary, help. When the dog has complied, reward the dog by telling it to jump to the spot you chose to share. In the end, the dog gets to share your "space" but it is not confused about who is in control of that space.

The ritual of feeding a dog is one of great importance and should be taken very seriously. Dogs who are allowed to graze from their food dish throughout the day believe that they are providing or "hunting" their own food. This begs the question: If they are providing their own food, what do they need you for? Second, if they are the providers of the food, being responsible for or protecting that "kill" is their natural right. This line of thought will eventually cultivate the dog's inherent aggressive side. By simply requiring a dog to sit before feeding changes the entire dynamic. You are then providing the food (as any viable pack leader would), and the dog's willingness to oblige by obeying your "sit" command completes the circle of the leader/follower relationship. Having had a working relationship with man for the better part of the last 25,000 years, the dog really does prefer it this way. This is the single, most important change in daily routine for a dog showing even the slightest aggressive tendency.

Madeline then asked why the dogs preferred to eat only after the two women arrived home in the evening. I explained that one of the responsibilities of dog(s) who are in charge of their pack is to keep that pack together. Eating is a ritual that is carried out when the entire group is present, so once the women arrived home and the pack was again whole, the dogs were free to begin the ritual of mealtime (with the dogs eating first, in the order of the hierarchy as they were perceiving it!).

As I continued to explain, the expressions on both women's faces changed to pleased comprehension, as so often happens when one locates the missing piece of a jigsaw puzzle. When we break down aspects of behavior bit by bit, it is far easier to distinguish what is really going on.

It seemed that Bonnie, who was raised (with so many other dogs) in the tranquility of the country, was simply not prepared for city life. This explained her fearful, predatory behavior on the street. She was, however (having been raised with other dogs), prepared for her relationship with Clyde. So prepared, in fact, that she quickly taught him to follow her behavioral patterns and her responses to various stimuli. This was the basis for Clyde's own recent lapse in manners. In addition, because dogs use their own excrement to mark ownership of a territory, permitting Bonnie to eliminate in the house encouraged her to become even more territorial than before. This resulted in her lack of social grace with visitors. Clyde, once again, was content to follow her lead.

The two dogs spent their daylight hours together, reinforcing their bond to each other as a pack of two. Once the women arrived home, the dogs found it hard to readjust to a pack of four. And, because the women ignored the tenets of basic obedience, the dogs assumed that they (the dogs) were in charge. Allowing the dogs on higher ground (i.e., letting them on the furniture or carrying Bonnie in the street instead of requiring her to walk) and allowing them to eat at will served to put the proverbial nail in their behavioral coffins.

Figuring out the problem—which we had just done—is always the first step in figuring out the solution. It was now time to make the necessary corrections to everyone's behavior. First, Madeline and Katherine had to reestablish the order of hierarchy within the pack. That would, of course, be done through the practice of basic obedience and requiring the dogs to "work" for a living. This "work" would be the vehicle that helped them all understand their roles within the group. Each member of the group had a specific job description, and understanding these descriptions would eliminate any contests about who was in charge.

Madeline and Katherine were both bosses; they had equal power. Now conscious of the dynamic of pack hierarchy, Katherine's personality would ultimately and naturally emerge as stronger. (The dogs would sense this superiority and perform at a higher level for the stronger of the two humans). Nonetheless, basic obedience ("sit," "come," "down," "stay") sessions were to be practiced daily by both women. The length of the session was not important. The key here was follow-through. "If you tell the dogs to do something," I instructed them, "make sure they do it—even if you have to help." I also warned that each should be careful not to step in and finish a command the other had started. Because the dogs already sensed who (of the two humans) was really "top dog," they would be even less inclined to listen to the second-in-command if the stronger personality always stepped in to help. So, whoever started the command was to follow through and finish it.

This exercise could initially be done with a food treat (a reward), but only as a reintroduction to the world of "You please me, I please you." After that (with the exception of mealtimes), verbal praise would be sufficient. This, of course, included telling the dogs "off" whenever they jumped to higher ground such as the couch or a chair, followed by the command "sit." Then—and only then—were they to be praised for following an order, and at that point they could be told to come up again as a reward for following commands.

Once the dogs' "language" skills were sufficiently sharpened, each dog should then be assigned a designated "relaxation" spot (i.e., a towel, a pillow, a dog bed, etc.).

Both dogs were to be told several times a day to "go to your place" and be instructed to "down-stay." The length of time the dogs were to remain in the "down-stay" was initially to be no more than a few seconds and eventually lengthened to several minutes. Once this exercise was no longer a game of fetching and replacing the dogs as they slunk away from their beds, Katherine and Madeline could begin adding distraction to the recipe.

Now, every time the phone rang, the dogs were told to "go to your place" and "down-stay." They were to "stay" for however long the phone call lasted. Once the phone call was over and the receiver back on the hook, the dogs were to be praised and then released from the "down-stay." The objective here was to teach the dogs to relax while distracted. The "down-stay" exercise is designed to force the dogs to be still even though their first inclination is to get up and start "running interference" at the slightest hint of an intrusive noise. Eventually, this same exercise was to be done when the doorbell rang and, even farther down the road, if a visitor came to call.

As for Bonnie's "street scenes," I recommended that she be carried from the apartment to wherever the destination of the walk was to be. If it was just a "bathroom" walk for Clyde, then the distance might be only a few blocks. She was to be put down only when they were headed home. As she was preoccupied with "getting inside" anyway, her focus would then be on getting home with as little distraction, and as quickly, as possible.

Not only would she be learning to walk on the street (hopefully without incident) but she would be successful at it as well—having been put down and walked home all on her own. Dogs are very proud of their successes and want to repeat them. The object here was to convince Bonnie that she really could walk through the "sea of legs" and still make it to her desired destination. Praising her quietly while she walked would help her to relax as well. If she happened to stop along the way to eliminate, all the better. The less she went to the bathroom in the house, the less territorial she would feel the need to be when visitors were in her home.

Now, for the last and most important part of the task in helping these dogs to relax. If you want to convince a dog that you are the leader of its pack, make that dog work for its food. It sounds easier than it actually is because most of us associate food with love. If we feed the dog, then it will love us. The small detail we often leave out of this equation is the way we feed the dog. This is, in fact, very important to the dog. As I mentioned earlier in this chapter, if you just put the food down and walk away, you no longer (from the dog's perspective) have anything to do with the actual feeding. Therefore, you must tell the dog to sit and then feed it. Requiring even a simple "sit" changes the entire ritual of feeding from the dog being in charge to you being in charge. The tough part of the exercise occurs if the dog does not sit. Should this happen, you must simply throw the meal away and leave the room.

I have yet to meet a dog lover who can do this with ease. More often than not, guilt forces you to ask the dog to sit several times; this negates the exercise entirely. If you can, however, show the dog (often only once) that you will not feed him unless he obeys you, he will simply obey you. Both women were eager to assume their new roles as "pack leaders" and agreed, albeit reluctantly, to follow through even at mealtimes. Katherine, Madeline, and I discussed one more option that we all agreed would help their dogs: "doggy day care." I admit that it sounds a bit silly, but don't be fooled by the whimsical label. This is a serious alternative to your dog pining away at home alone. If Bonnie and Clyde, instead of being alone together all day were exposed to a dog environment that was run by humans, the evening transition from dog/dog pack to dog/human pack would be a snap. And on top of that, they would be tired at the end of the day, just like Katherine and Madeline.

In a few short weeks, Bonnie and Clyde had begun to make great strides. They were staying "down" on their respective beds whenever they were told and, on the whole, were relaxing more. Visitors who came to call felt a lot less threatened when the dogs were watching from afar. Mealtime became the most rewarding part of the day, and both dogs ate whenever they were fed, never leaving even a morsel in their bowls. Now, whenever one of the dogs wants to join Katherine or Madeline on the couch, they sit and wait until they are invited to leave the ground.

Bonnie's fearful behavior on the street has improved but is far from gone. This transition will take the most work, as she was imprinted at a young age to live in the peace and quiet of the country. She can now, however, successfully make it home from doggy day care, which is several blocks away.

Both women noticed that their dogs had become, on the whole, far more relaxed, and that their behavior had improved dramatically. They were easier to be around as their behavior became less erratic and far more predictable. They were well socialized and supervised at day care, and tired enough when they all arrived home in the evening that the entire pack (women and dogs) welcomed the downtime. Bonnie and Clyde clearly preferred being the less responsible members of the pack. Reaping the benefits as a worker seemed far easier for these dogs than dealing with the responsibilities that come with being boss.

Thankfully, Bonnie and Clyde have left far fewer impressions of their teeth on anyone's legs since our work together began. Having the dogs in a "down-stay" whenever visitors arrive has helped them—and the visitors—to relax. It is always less stressful for a dog if they know where they belong in a given situation, rather than running around helter-skelter trying to find a spot for themselves. There was, however, one incident with a workman in Madeline and Katherine's weekend house. It seems his tool belt (with all of its dangling, noisy weapons) was too much for Bonnie to bear. But, thanks to the workman's choice of heavyweight jeans and Katherine's diligent eye on her dog, the "play" was quickly intercepted and the "pass" rendered incomplete. Bonnie got two minutes in her dog bed as a penalty for the "foul."

Bonnie and Clyde are just two of the tens of millions of dogs who are trying to send messages to their human pack members. Whether living in the quiet of suburbia or the electric excitement of a city, the dynamics of your relationship with your dog will greatly weigh on the results of your dog's behavior toward others. So, wherever you reside, if you are having a hard time living with your dog, the chances are that your dog is having a hard time living with you.

Not all dog behavior can be modified with training techniques alone. In a perfect world, perhaps, but it would be unrealistic to believe that all dogs are created equal. Many have been abused, neglected, or simply irresponsibly bred. Dog breeding can be a crap game of genetic science, and it's rare to meet a genetic scientist who is also a dog breeder. (Actually, I did find one and I purchased a wonderful dog from her. But that was sheer luck.)

Most breeders are very careful to choose temperament as the most important factor in dog reproduction and—as many of us who have beautiful, healthy dogs know—it is possible to breed beauty with sound temperament. But beauty is often the temptress that wins over temperament—after all, the prettier the doggy in the window, the faster it sells. For those of us who have chosen one of these pretty faces as a soul mate, with little knowledge of their soundness of mind, hang on, you're in for a bumpy ride.

A dog who has been abused or whose temperament has been traded for good looks can be a dog owner's worst nightmare. Many of these mistreated or poorly bred dogs need help in letting down their "guard" if their behavior is to be modified at all. Enter the science of pharmacology. Just as humans can be helped with behavioral drugs, so can dogs. Modern medicine has produced a veritable treasure chest of psychoactive drugs that, when administered properly (only by a veterinarian), can often make an enormous difference in the ultimate result of a dog's fate.

Finding the proper drug and the accurate dose is no easy task, but a good veterinarian, preferably with a background in animal behavior, who is willing to work in conjunction with a professional trainer, as well as the dog's own family, is often the only alternative with a dog that is otherwise unreachable through conventional methods alone. For years, many people have had a hard time with this idea and many dogs who could otherwise have been helped were not. Happily, the modern dog owner seems to be coming around.

With a wealth of information literally at our fingertips, the average consumer is becoming an educated consumer. With "quality of life" prevailing in most households as the mantra of the new millennium, dog lovers are now willing to admit that stress, even for our dogs, can cause anyone to "snap."

Come In, Said the Spider to the Fly . . .

Simon was, without a doubt, the most breathtakingly beautiful standard poodle I had ever seen. He held himself in such a way that one couldn't help but stare before approaching him in greeting. If he were a man, he could easily have been an Armani runway model. Simon's owner, Meghan, an entertainment attorney, had asked me to help with what she referred to as "Simon's alter ego." This otherwise enormously friendly dog, it seemed, had a Jekyll-Hyde personality.

He was five years old and, for quite some time, he had been impossible to walk on the streets. He had what seemed like an insatiable need to have a physical confrontation with just about every dog he saw. Walking him was, to say the least, extremely unpleasant and restraining him was both nearly impossible and utterly exhausting. Once inside, however, he was easygoing and mild-mannered. He enjoyed having guests come to visit but, on occasion, seemed guarded as they moved about the house. Sometimes he would greet a guest with great enthusiasm and then, for no apparent reason, would change his posture to suspicion toward that same guest.

Gradually, his behavior became more erratic. He would become almost hysterical whenever the doorbell rang. After months of enduring his explosive episodes, Meghan found it easier to lock him up in her room, let her guest(s) in, and then bring Simon out. This seemed far easier for him to cope with. It was as if, Meghan said, her dog was not sure if he loved the company or he hated it.

The day came, however, when during one of Meghan's many dinner parties, a guest got up from the table to make a phone call. Simon was resting somewhere near the table and, as the guest passed him, the dog ignited into a charge and bit the man on the leg. Thankfully, very little damage was done to the man's leg. Then, as quickly and inexplicably as he had detonated, Simon retreated back to his resting place almost as if in shame. Meghan was mortified and could only believe this bizarre behavior was an isolated incident. Unfortunately, she was wrong.

In the months that followed, Simon's behavior became even more troubling. Whenever Meghan was out of the house, the dog would spend his days hiding in an upstairs closet. His appetite waned and he almost always left his food in the dish, uneaten. Only when Meghan came home would he come out of the closet. He ran down the stairs with great enthusiasm and, once he saw her, acted like a very normal, happy dog. If, however, it was not Meghan but, instead, the housekeeper, or Meghan's boyfriend, Simon would go only as far as the first-floor landing, see that it was not Meghan, and run back up to his closet lair.

The breaking point came when Meghan's sister came to stay for a long weekend. She had known Simon since he was a pup and their relationship was solid and healthy. It was the day after she arrived and she was getting ready to go out for the afternoon. She had spent the morning playing with Simon, out in the garden, and hadn't noticed that he had gone off somewhere to rest. She ran upstairs to change her clothes and as she reached into the closet—BANG!—out shot Simon, teeth and all. By the time she realized what had happened, the dog was cowering in the corner in shame. Meghan's heart was broken, not only for her sister, but because she knew something was seriously wrong with her dog. That's when Meghan got my number from a friend and we made an appointment to meet.

After complimenting her on her beautiful dog, I began to ask my standard list of questions. Meghan was able to give me a wealth of information that would undoubtedly help lead to the cause of at least some of Simon's problems. She had purchased the dog (from a pet shop) when he was only seven weeks old. For the first three years of Simon's life with Meghan they shared a house, a bed, and just about all of Meghan's leisure time. Simon knew his basic obedience commands and, as poodles can be amazingly intelligent and inherently stubborn, with a few exceptions he was a brilliant student. So brilliant, in fact, that Meghan didn't feel the need to keep current with his obedience work as he clearly understood everything the woman said. Meghan mentioned that she loved that they ate breakfast together in the morning. She would put Simon's food down and then get her own breakfast. They always ate together, at least in the morning.

He was a natural puller whenever he was attached to a leash. He liked always to be ahead of Meghan on their walks. Meghan said, "It was as if he was making sure that the path ahead of them was safe for her to walk." He liked to play with other dogs but made sure to dominate them before playing.

It was just after Simon turned three that Meghan began a serious relationship with a man. He sometimes spent the night, but usually not more than two times weekly. At first, Simon objected (by way of a growl) to being thrown out of the only bed he had ever known. Eventually, Meghan found it more comfortable, on the nights when her friend stayed over, to take Simon into another room while they slept. Eventually, after several confrontational moments with Meghan's boyfriend, Simon realized he was no longer going to be the man in her bed and he accepted (albeit grudgingly) the new pack member.

The house had a spacious outdoor garden so, whenever the weather was inclement, Meghan chose not to take Simon for a long walk and, instead, allowed the dog to use the garden as a bathroom. As Simon became more antisocial on his outdoor walks, Meghan required him to use the garden more frequently. Meghan did not realize that the less social Simon was required to be, the more antisocial he was becoming.

There were so many forces in play here that it was understandably difficult to see the forest for the trees. To begin with, Simon was very content as a "pack of two" and the addition (or intrusion, as Simon probably saw it) of another pack member threw off the dynamics of Simon's frame of mind. Whenever Meghan's boyfriend did not stay over, Simon was welcomed in his old spot on the bed. This inconsistency forced him to "face off" with Meghan's boyfriend every time he stayed at the house. He also made a clear connection with being thrown out of bed only on the nights Meghan had "the visitor." Simon then began to see all guests (who he had once viewed as a welcome commodity) as potential intruders on his precious one-on-one time with Meghan.

Because he felt the need to retreat to his closet lair whenever Meghan was out of the house, a walk outside (on the busy streets of New York) in the evening was perceived as even more competition—this time with dogs as well as people—and made Simon even more tense. Because dogs communicate first with body language, being attached to a four- or a six-foot leash didn't make matters any easier. Whether it was another dog approaching Simon or Simon approaching another dog, somehow the leashes prohibited them from sending clear signals back and forth. One misinterpreted body message was all Simon needed to "put up his dukes." This forced Meghan to allow Simon to use the house garden even more frequently. It was shortly after that that the dog's unpredictable behavior with guests began.

It is important to note that a dog eliminates not only to relieve its body of the pressure of waste but also to claim ownership of a specific territory. Meghan's decision to allow Simon to use the garden as a toilet only strengthened his conviction that the house itself belonged to him and, therefore, a guest of Meghan's was, to Simon, now an intruder. This further explained his change in behavior toward those he had once freely allowed to visit.

Was it possible that the love Meghan felt for her dog—the love that initially prompted her to indulge him (i.e., not require him to work for her affection or for rewards)—was the same love that had forced her to isolate him (after the first biting incident) in order to protect him? If that was the case, then it would only make sense that Simon's love for Meghan and his need (via the messages he received while she was indulging him) to be a strong, protective pack leader began to conflict with his need to be social, thereby forcing him to make a choice between Meghan and the outside world.

Once he chose Meghan (as any dog would have), the stage had been set for the disasters that followed. And to make matters even worse, the increasing impulse to isolate the dog (which was initially designed to protect him) was at the very core of Simon's increasing volatility.

So, how should Meghan handle this situation? We mapped out a behavioral-modification routine that included more socialization through outdoor exercise, daily formal obedience lessons, the long "down-stay," and requiring Simon to sit and stay for his meals (one of which was to be fed by Meghan's boyfriend).

Obviously, Simon's behavioral problems were more extreme—and more potentially dangerous—than those of some of the previously discussed dogs. Meghan and I also talked about the very real possibility that Simon needed more help than even the most complex training techniques could provide. In order for this dog to relax, even if only enough to let us work on changing his behavior, he would undoubtedly need the help of modern pharmacology. Meghan agreed.

The first step in determining what drug would be most helpful for Simon would require a thorough blood test to ensure that he was physically sound. Then Meghan's veterinarian (after discussing the details of Simon's behavioral problems) would determine the drug and its dose. In this particular case, the medication chosen was Prozac.

Behavioral modification began immediately, and the Prozac began to take effect after about two weeks. Both prescriptions have worked wonders with this dog, but the reality is that he must be constantly socialized, constantly reminded of who is in charge, and constantly watched. Leaving him to his own devices would undoubtedly lead to serious trouble.

One of the things that Meghan and I found particularly helpful was putting down a bed for Simon in the living room. Directly behind the bed we screwed a large eye hook into the wall onto which a leash could be affixed. Simon was taught to "go to his place" several times a day (much like Bonnie and Clyde). When guests were in the house, he was tethered with a leash to the eye hook as a safety measure.

Simon's walks are now split between Meghan, her boyfriend, and a professional dog walker. Each is aware that the dog is not just out there to walk, but also to work. In Simon's case, the main objective has been to teach the dog to focus on the walker instead of on the hunt. If Simon met with the slightest bit of success during his walk—if he made eye contact, for example—his walker lavished him with praise and sometimes even a treat. He does, however, wear a soft cloth muzzle as another safety precaution. With months of labor-intensive behavioral and environmental retraining (on Meghan's part), and exercise as well as modern medicine (eventually the dog was weaned from the medication), I am relieved to say that Simon is a much happier dog. He no longer spends his days hiding in a closet and has returned to Meghan's dinner gatherings as the life of the party. With the addition of a "Gentle Leader" (a halterlike collar that fits around the dog's muzzle, enabling the walker to control the dog's body by way of controlling its head), his behavior with other dogs has also improved. Simon no longer feels the need to spar with every dog he sees; it seems that he needs to do so only with the first dog he sees. After that, it's simply a walk in the park.

With so many of our beloved canine companions behaving more like snapping turtles than dogs, a closer look at natural dog behavior can always help to shed light on what too often ends up being the downfall of the man/dog relationship.

Dogs are direct descendants of the wolf and need (like the wolf) to exist within an established pack hierarchy. Inconsistencies (usually in the form of indulgences) within this hierarchy become fodder for confusion. A confused dog always feels challenged to prove itself as strong and useful. These challenges can be with people as well as other dogs, and they take place indoors as well as outdoors.

Often, when a dog is confrontational with other dogs, he is merely trying to establish a relationship. Many "dog fights" are not really dog fights at all, but are "dog conversations." It is through these body dances (which we sometimes perceive as fights) that one dog is able to find out about another dog—sort of a resumé or audition, if you will. If two dogs happen to be an equal energy match and neither is quick to submit, the dance may get a bit rougher and last a bit longer but, if more people would force themselves to stand back and let the dogs have a moment to "speak dog," the "introduction" might not have to be repeated the next time the two dogs meet.

Many social off-leash dogs often become less social once their leashes are snapped on. Perhaps it is a combination of restricted movement and being attached to the pack member for whom the dog thinks he is responsible that turns a dog from social butterfly to firecracker with the snap of a buckle.

To say that all dogs are sufficiently reliable to be allowed off-leash during social interaction would be irresponsible at best. However, to ignore the huge difference—from a dog's perspective—in being on- or off-leash would be like throwing away the clue that could potentially solve many behavioral mysteries. For a dog to be tethered to the end of a four- or a six-foot line would be roughly the equivalent, for humans, of being handcuffed. That your communication skills would suffer pretty much goes without saying. A little slackening of everybody's line might help a lot.

With the number of dogs having sensitive personalities rising quickly, and wide-open spaces becoming rare commodities, responsible dog owners need to be aware of their dog-care options and, even more important, open to new ideas.

As modern science and technology offer options that allow us to help our dogs as never before, and luxuries like day care and dog walkers add even further to the menu of choices, exploring these options is a small price to pay for the health and well-being of a dog. Be careful, however, not to overdo. Too much of a good thing has also been known to backfire now and again.

Doggy day care has its advantages, but too much time around other canines might just teach your dog to become more competitive with them. Just as you would seek out the best veterinarian to help determine if medication is an option for your dog, be sure also to keep in close touch with the caregivers who monitor your dog's daily behavior. After all, one can never be too careful when raising a latchkey dog.

For the dog who feels the need to meet and greet with his mouth, several head halters are now available (on the retail market) to help give dog owners better control of their dogs. As newfangled as they look, their design is based on the age-old concept of the equine halter. Their construction neutralizes the pulling power of the dog and allows the walker the freedom to change the dog's focus by leading him around by the nose. If your dog is lunging at other dogs, the head collar allows you the option of turning your dog's head to focus on you instead of on the source of aggravation. You'd be surprised by how helpful this can be.

Canines are territorial creatures that do not view public space as "public" at all, but as territory to be claimed. With populations (dog and human) on the rise, it should not be surprising that more and more dogs are getting into turf disputes. Teaching your dog to focus more on you and less on outside distractions is the best medicine here.

Being a creative and well-informed dog owner will help you find the alternatives and remedies needed to make your dog's surroundings easier for him to deal with. If expensive day care or dog walkers are not an option, try enlisting the help of a neighbor or a student who might be interested in keeping company with or exercising your dog for at least a part of the day.

Remember to provide strong leadership (when you are with the dog), thus freeing the dog of the burden of doing so. Even the most subtle changes in a dog's life can help him to relax in a stressful situation.

Dogs are constantly watching and waiting for signs from other pack members to determine the "temperature" of a given situation. If you are nervous about your dog's behavior in the street, nine times out of ten that dog will sense your anxiety and will act accordingly. By the same token, if you are rushing, then you are probably rushing your dog. Often, teaching yourself to relax will help your dog to relax.

When we are upset, we raise our voices. Dogs growl. A growl, however, is more often than not a precursor to a bite. Growling and biting are all parts of a dog's natural way of sending messages. If you were a dog, you would understand these messages. Dogs don't like to get into physical fights any more than we do; that's why they growl first. But, if you don't practice "dog-speak" and the growl goes unheeded, you might just get bitten. And, to the dog, you've actually asked for the bite.

Sometimes dogs bite because they are not well, but more often it's a signal that they are uneasy about a specific situation. Whether it is fear that prompts a dog to bite, a natural predatory response, or just good, old-fashioned territoriality, biting is just one of the ways a dog sends a message about how it is feeling. Understandable though it may be, aggression in any form is obviously unacceptable.

As I've stressed throughout this book, along with the joys of living with a dog comes a great deal of responsibility. The responsibility of being a patient and consistent leader for your dog is paramount. Training, nutrition, exercise, and socialization follow as the necessary ingredients to raising and living with any dog. Keeping in mind that dog aggression—while instinctive—is never acceptable in a dog's daily routine will help you to keep yourself in check as an effective dog leader.

We have become a society of dog owners who no longer require our dogs to *do what we say* but, ask instead, *let us know what you want*. In spite of this, dogs want what they've always wanted—the satisfaction of serving a strong leader. Dogs are a species of workers that we no longer require to work, and long-term unemployment is always unpleasant.

The bottom line is this: If we continue to allow, and even require, our dogs to run our "packs," then they (the dogs) will understandably act like dogs. But if we instead expect them to behave like good citizens, then we must first teach *them* to follow *our* lead.

Chapter 6

The Brat Pack

Spoiled Dogs

Just last week I saw a woman in New York City walking her dogs—only the dogs weren't walking. The woman was pulling them around in a wagon! One of the dogs, a pug, was dressed in a black velvet collar bedecked with faux jewels. The collar was so big that I overheard a little girl ask her father as they passed, "Daddy, why is that little dog wearing a pillow around its neck?" I'm not certain how the woman planned to let the dogs go to the bathroom. I imagined that, as the wagon approached an acceptable spot, the woman might lift the dogs up over the sidewalk and

*allow them to eliminate in midair. I must confess, I
laughed out loud as I thought to myself, "This gives
new meaning to the phrase 'Do you want to go out?' "*

Admittedly, the modern dog has had to make quite a few lifestyle adjustments in order to continue to keep company with modern man—it's no
wonder these dogs are beginning to resemble a pack of spoiled, though
still adorable, brats. It's hard not to notice the frightening comparison
with the way we are raising our modern children—all with a sense of
entitlement and no self-control. However, if you were ushered around
in a Sherpa bag, had your very own treat dispenser, got less aerobic
exercise than a stuffed dog, rarely saw the people you thought you were
living with, and had more couture accessories than a runway model, you
might be a little full of yourself, too.

We have all, at some point in our lives, either lived with, known, or
at the very least witnessed the behavior of a member of what might be
called the "brat pack." These are the dogs who seem perpetually
annoyed. The slightest change in plans will send them into a full-blown
tailspin. These dogs are intolerant of strangers and impatient with their
peers. They ignore direction and become insolent when challenged.
Their entire persona is reminiscent of a spoiled child and, as is usually
the case, we, their beloved guardians, are more than a little responsible
for these bad attitudes.

Whatever our reasons (and they range from the ridiculous to the
sublime), the song remains the same. Dog lovers far and wide are sub-
stituting loving indulgence for the basic elements of good citizenship.
In other words, we are encouraging disrespect and insolence and we are
ending up with creatures that are disrespectful and insolent. Whoever
coined the phrase "love is blind" was undoubtedly referring to their own
"brat" dog. The truth is, no one who has ever picked up a leash is
immune to indulging a badly behaved dog—not even me.

As a mother, I have sometimes found myself overindulging my children (and my dogs) in order to soothe some feeling of guilt or inade-
quacy that comes from balancing motherhood with a career. Their
appreciation of my generosity is, I am sorry to say, more often than not

boldly disingenuous, leaving me with an even greater need to indulge them yet again.

As I peer further into the lives of those people who are trying to legitimately attain the perfect balance between canine companionship and canine ownership, I find that this meliorative impulse is universal: More and more of us follow schedules that allow downtime for little more than sleep. With a Filofax full of appointments and daily agendas that resemble a complex football play, we are left with precious little time for the dog and a more than ample load of guilt.

It is this guilt, coupled with the fact that the dog now often represents much more than a pet—our most valued possession; our child; our soul mate; the very glue that often holds our multifaceted lives together—that keeps us steadfastly on the path to overindulgence. So we continue our quest to find that one toy or that one treat or that one belly rub that might encourage the devotion we so deserve. But, sadly (although not surprisingly), as our pocketbooks and our patience wear thin, our charge's behavior toward us (and the rest of the world) only becomes worse. How can they be so ungrateful—after all, haven't we given them everything they could possibly want?

Regardless of the species, when parenting, one must be very careful not to cross the line from caretaker to servant. Dogs everywhere are beginning to let us know through their misbehavior that far too many of us humans are acting like attendants rather than masters. Wealth, to a dog, is not measured in dollars and cents, but instead in the strength and security of knowing who is in charge. Confusion is just one result of indulging a dog. Another result is canine behavior that very closely resembles that of a spoiled child.

Brat dogs come in all shapes and sizes and live in the most unlikely places—places like your house and my house. Many of them balk at the prospect of a simple walk on the street and others snarl when you reach to scoop them up for a quick peck on the snout. Some grumble at passerby who stop to admire their beauty, while others stare blankly at you when you lovingly request that they follow a command. Identifying them is easier than living with them but, take heart, because even a member of the infamous brat pack can be transformed into a well-mannered citizen of the canine kind.

If we (the people) continue to use them (the dogs) as vehicles for soothing our own discontent, we will eventually create the ultimate brat dog—a dog who will barely tolerate even the people it lives with. But, if we could learn to hold our dogs in the highest esteem while at the same time treating them like the dogs they are, fewer and fewer of these difficult dogs would ever feel the need to act like brats at all.

Got Milk?

Believed to have been around since before the seventh century, the Pekingese is a breed of dog which, highly regarded by the Chinese imperial family, was treated as a sacred, royal treasure. Polo would have fit right in.

Bridgette, a woman who I believe to be in her mid to late fifties, was an enviably "well-preserved" woman who took pride in her strikingly beautiful appearance. Her dog, a two-year old Pekingese named Polo, was equally striking and, like his owner, carried himself with pride. The two, needless to say, attracted quite a bit of attention wherever they went.

I had worked with Bridgette and Polo when Polo was about eleven months old. The dog had begun to show signs of intolerance toward family members, as well as toward people outside the house. Bridgette had become concerned. She thought that her dog might be unhappy and wanted to do everything necessary to ensure Polo's contentment. Like the Chinese imperial family (more than thirteen centuries ago), Bridgette also held her dog in the highest regard.

Polo shared a house with Bridgette, Bridgette's husband, Jack, and two full-time housekeepers named Anna and Rose. Anna was in charge of the dog's morning meal, which consisted of boiled chicken and brown rice, and Rose was responsible for Polo's evening meal, steamed fish and brown rice. Both women prepared the respective meals and served them in porcelain dishes, but fed them to the dog, for the most part, by hand.

Although there were dog beds in nearly every room in the house, Polo preferred to sleep on Bridgette and Jack's bed—more specifically, on Jack's pillow. Bridgette often took Polo "out to lunch" with her and, because the Pekingese has a particularly long fur coat, Bridgette chose to carry Polo rather than let him walk on the "dirty" streets. The dog was paper trained, and generally used Bridgette's bathroom as his toilet.

When Polo was about eight months old, he began to show less and less interest in his meals. Bridgette thought he might be bored with the menu, so the bill of fare was changed to scrambled eggs in the morning and lamb in the evening. When this didn't work, Bridgette tried feeding Polo by hand, but without much success. Finally, Bridgette tried feeding Polo by hand in the marital bed. Soon after that, Polo began to growl at Jack whenever he tried to get into bed at night. Being the good dog owner that he was, Jack took to sleeping in the guest room, allowing Polo his place beside his wife, pillow and all.

One afternoon, while lunching together in a local café, Polo snapped at a waiter who was reaching down to pet him as he relaxed in Bridgette's arms. Bridgette was horrified but explained that the dog didn't like to be disturbed while resting. On several occasions after that, Polo snapped at people who stopped to admire him on the street. He was, of course, always in Bridgette's arms when this happened, and Bridgette explained that Polo didn't like to be touched by strangers.

The woman began to worry that her dog was truly unhappy. How, she wondered, having done everything humanly possible to tend to all of Polo's needs, could he possibly be unhappy? Bridgette was not easily discouraged, however, so she went out and bought Polo a new collar and leash and several new toys. Polo was not, as you might have already suspected, placated. But it wasn't until he snapped at the veterinarian during a routine checkup that the vet advised Bridgette to enlist the help of a trainer. This is where I came in.

After describing, in great detail, "a day in the life of Polo," Bridgette asked if I thought there was anything she could do to help her dog be happy. "Yes," I replied, "treat him like a dog." Bridgette looked as if I had informed her that Polo was going to die. The prospect of treating this "little treasure" like a "dog" was more than she could bear. Before I could say another word, Bridgette practically shouted: "I don't think I can do it!"

Plainly, this was not what Bridgette wanted to hear. She tried one last-ditch effort to deter me from the course of such evil advice. "Some time ago," she said, "I read in a book that thousands of years ago, Pekingese were regarded as treasures. They were raised with such great care that they even had their own wet nurses. Do you think Polo might have suffered some kind of emotional loss because of never having had a wet nurse?"

As I could offer nothing even resembling a reasonable answer to such a shockingly odd question, I immediately steered the conversation back to more familiar ground. Dogs, I explained, regardless of their genetic lineage or breed history, need to be related to on a level they can understand. No matter how a dog is pampered, even to excess, it must be done in such a way that the dog can absorb your response to a given behavior. Once you lose your dog's concerned attention, you have lost the art of communicating with your dog.

I continued to explain. Allowing herself to think that Polo needed more than he actually did to lead a contented existence had brought Bridgette and the dog to a state of utter chaos. It had also been the catalyst for Polo's unattractive behavior.

It took a great deal of convincing, but Bridgette finally agreed to try a few behavioral techniques that I suggested might put Polo in better spirits. Initially, I wasn't so sure that Bridgette could do it, but to my surprise and great delight, she stuck to the plan. The first thing to change was where and how Polo ate his meals. I couldn't even come close to convincing Bridgette to feed this dog actual dog food. However, I have learned a few things about working with people and their dogs—quit while you're ahead! So, we agreed that the menu stay but the manner in which it was served be changed. Both Polo's A.M. and P.M. meals were to be fed in his food dishes (not by hand!) and were to be fed on the kitchen floor. They could initially be left down as long as an hour (even little dogs don't need all day to finish a meal) but, after that, whatever remained in the dish was to be thrown away. Eventually, the food was to be taken up sooner. No matter what (I stressed to Bridgette), this dog was not to be fed outside the kitchen and must absolutely not be fed by hand. Bridgette grudgingly agreed. Next came obedience lessons. It wasn't necessary for Polo to know more than two or three commands, but it was imperative that he have some language in common with his people. I stressed that Jack and the housekeepers were to use the same training words as Bridgette in order to sustain continuity for the dog. We chose "sit," "stay," and "down." Initially, Bridgette and I did this together with Polo but, after that, she and the rest of the family needed to practice it on their own, in three-to-five-minute sessions, as many times a day as possible. It wasn't necessary to teach Polo how to "come," as he was almost always in Bridgette's arms anyway. That little tidbit of information led us straight to the next step of our task.

I explained to Bridgette that a large part of her dog's problem lay in the fact that he was always being held, touched, or catered to in some fashion or another. There is a time and a place for everything, and dogs—even when grooming one another—have practical reasons for physical contact. In Polo's case, he had far too much physical contact. He simply needed some space!

To begin with, Bridgette needed to let Polo walk on his own—yes, even on the dirty streets. I suggested that she simply have him bathed more often, and this seemed to appeal to her. I explained that, when in her arms, the dog not only felt bigger and stronger than he actually was, but probably also felt the need to snap at anyone trying to "separate" him from Bridgette. Although Bridgette had actually found this behavior rather endearing, once she understood what it represented, she agreed to try letting him walk on the ground instead.

With these three lifestyle changes (applied separately and then eventually combined), Polo has become a great deal more pleasant to be around. He still goes out to lunch with Bridgette, but he now walks to the restaurant and, instead of sitting on Bridgette's lap, he sits in his own chair. (Letting him sit on the floor was out of the question for Bridgette.) Now, whenever someone approaches Polo on the street, Bridgette commands him to "sit." He is grateful for the attention he receives and perceives it as a reward for sitting. Because he no longer has to be on his guard, he no longer snaps at admirers.

As for his meals, Polo now "sits" and "stays" before he is fed and, except for the occasional eggshell accidentally caught in the scrambled eggs, he finishes just about everything he's given. Jack is grateful to be back in bed with his wife—and his dog. Polo still sleeps on Jack's pillow, which is now safely positioned at the foot of the bed. Jack sleeps on another pillow. Oh yes, one more thing. As for the wet nurse, Bridgette and I finally agreed that such a notion was meant for some other time, some other place, and some other dog.

. . .

Changing the way an animal lives, in order to make life less stressful for that animal, does not mean you love the animal any less. On the contrary, to the dog, it means you love him even more. Sending the proper psychological messages is the healthiest thing we can do for our dogs.

If more people were open to the concept that certain foods might not initially taste all that wonderful but are nonetheless healthier, more of us might try these foods and, as a result, be healthier. Similarly, if more people were open to the concept that treating your dog like a dog is far better for the dog, more of us might adopt this perspective for the sake of our dogs. Feeding healthy thoughts is as important as feeding healthy food.

The problems that ensue from misinterpreting our dogs' needs run the gamut from annoying to downright dangerous. What sometimes begins as a seemingly harmless love affair between man and dog often ends up as a partnership with the devil. There are, of course, always exceptions to this rule. If your dog is behaving in a fashion that pleases you and suits the way you live, then by all means don't fix what's not broken. But, if you begin to notice even the slightest signs of undesirable behavior, nipping such behavior in the bud is the best defense. The longer inappropriate behavior is tolerated, the more the dog interprets it as being acceptable, and the behavior then becomes habitual.

Because dogs automatically repeat behavior that they consider to be successful (i.e., if barking gets you to take them out, then they will bark when they want to go out), one must be extremely careful when indulging a dog not to inadvertently train "bad" behavior. This is the easiest of the many "love" traps that dog owners fall into but, thankfully, it is also one the easiest to get out of.

. . . Anything but a Boy Scout

I heard about Scout from a good friend who knew his owner and I so sympathized with his plight that I offered to help. Scout, a two-and-a-half-year-old soft-coated wheaton terrier, had become rather difficult to deal with and even more difficult to live with. Scout's owner, Sam, had adopted the dog from a shelter when Scout was approximately one year old. He was friendly to people, social (although sometimes overzealous) with other dogs, and extremely smart. Sam boasted that he hadn't really picked this dog but, in fact, this dog had picked him.

They sailed through the usual getting-to-know-you period with flying colors. Scout seemed to let Sam know just about everything he needed to. When the dog was hungry, he stood in the kitchen doorway and barked. Sam immediately fed him. If Scout wanted to go outside, he stood by the door and barked. Sam, of course, took him out. When Scout wanted to play, he would lie beside a pile of his many new toys (signaling playtime) and Sam would stop whatever he was doing, go and sit beside the dog, and play. Tug-of-war was the game of choice—more specifically, Scout's choice. When the dog was ready to "retire," he would retreat to Sam's bedroom, hop up on Sam's bed, and go to sleep.

Sam had never owned a dog before and he was thrilled with Scout. They seemed to connect immediately and Sam felt as though this dog was teaching him everything he needed to know about dogs. But, about six months after Scout had adopted Sam, the dog began to act in ways that the man could no longer understand. For instance, whenever Sam was home, Scout would nip at his hands. If Sam tried to tell the dog to stop, the nipping went from annoying to downright obnoxious.

On one occasion, Sam found a gaping hole in the arm of one of his living room chairs. At first he thought Scout could not have done it because he was never up on the living room chairs. The dog liked to chew his leash whenever he was out walking and Sam really didn't see the harm in it until, one day, as he inadvertently pulled the leash out of the dog's mouth, Scout reached up and bit his hand. Not a malicious bite, but one of impatience; Sam had simply not heeded the dog's desire to chew the leash. In order to stop Scout from biting him again, Sam now let the dog hold a toy in his mouth (instead of the leash) when they walked. Scout began to grumble at other dogs who passed him in the street and would even sometimes try to snap at them if they came anywhere near his mouth or his toy.

Scout also began to whine whenever Sam got ready to leave for work and, as Sam headed for the door, the dog would nip at his hands. One evening, as Sam approached his bed (with Scout already resting on top of it), the dog stood up and growled. Sam instantly threw the dog off the bed but quickly felt so bad about, not to mention a little frightened by, the confrontation that he invited Scout back up and they slept together curled up like spoons.

Having lost that blissful, heady feeling that one enjoys in the initial stages of a love affair with a dog, Sam did what any dog owner would do when faced with the overwhelming prospect that he hadn't a clue as to what to do about this dog's behavior, he bought a dog-training book. Then he bought another. Then he found a web site. When all this failed, he sent Scout away to obedience school for two weeks.

The school assured Sam that by the end of the two-week period Scout would be a new dog. They were right about that. When Sam went to pick up Scout, he was following commands (for them), staying sharply focused (on them), and generally acting like the dog they had promised to deliver. Only this new dog wasn't Sam's dog. Scout seemed to have no more motivation to work for him than he ever had. But, for the people who had retrained him to be a good citizen, he was, in fact, a new dog.

Sam went back to the proverbial drawing board and reread the books. Then he decided to try an obedience class that involved him as part of the equation. This proved to be rather successful whenever an instructor was standing over Sam's shoulder reminding him that he was the man and Scout the dog. But, alas, Sam confessed that the moment they got home—without someone prodding him on—he fell back into the same old patterns—and so did Scout.

By the time I came into the picture, Scout was practically holding Sam hostage in his own home. Sam said he felt weak and defeated. I explained that the dog undoubtedly knew this. I also explained that the problem was more likely one of miscommunication. Sam simply didn't have the "pack mentality." Scout needed to know who was in charge and Sam needed to know that love reigned supreme. Scout needed to know that he was useful and Sam needed to know that he was taking care of his dog. Two different species with very different needs. It's easy to see how this soup got so thick. Once the hierarchical pack mentality began to be enforced, I was certain that this relationship could be saved.

Sam had, believe it or not, committed almost all of the cardinal sins of dog ownership and had done so within the first few weeks of adopting Scout. To begin with, Sam had not established a single boundary in their relationship. This left the door wide open for the dog to set the parameters. Unfortunately, those the dog chose were of the "I bark and you jump" variety. In following Scout's orders (i.e., walking him when he wanted to be walked, feeding him when he wanted to be fed), Sam had confirmed to Scout that he was not willing to take charge—or in terms of pack mentality, not willing to challenge Scout's power.

Allowing the dog to initiate and conclude play sessions was just another ingredient in this disastrous recipe. Then came the icing on the cake, in the form of allowing this dog on "higher ground." (Remember Bonnie and Clyde in chapter 5?) Sam should not have been surprised that the dog felt compelled to own one of the living room chairs; after all, he already owned the bed. The nipping, whining, and snarling were simply Scout's way of communicating his dissatisfaction with his subordinate pack member. I was actually surprised that this dog didn't misbehave even more. Sam explained, in defense of his own actions, that he had read so many conflicting opinions on how to remedy his problems with Scout that he'd ended up in a muddle. I advised him to try to clear his head. Knowledge is power, yes, but too much knowledge can actually undermine power. Throw in a good dose of emotion and the plan is usually sabotaged altogether.

Dogs need precious little to survive and not much more than that to flourish: Some food, water, exercise, affection, and a job. The most prudent and effective way to help a dog become a member of the canine well mannered is to employ what is sometimes referred to as the "no-free-lunch" technique. I advised Sam that the easiest way to employ this program was to start over, as if he had just brought the dog home for the first time. I said this because it might help Sam to start over emotionally as well—without all the frustrations attached to his already failed attempts.

As with all dogs, Scout needed to learn some basic obedience commands and, as with all dogs, Scout needed to "work" for a living. This meant that all food (of any kind) and affection (of any kind) was to be given only as payment for the dog listening to the man. The first word Scout needed to learn was "off," and whenever he left the ground, for any reason, Sam was to command the dog "off" and gently but firmly help him to keep all four paws squarely on the ground. Because it wasn't a good idea for Sam to challenge Scout once he was safely ensconced on higher ground, I suggested he not allow the dog on higher ground in the first place. If he did, however, find the dog, say, for instance, already on the bed, so be it. Going into another room and whistling or making an interesting noise—thereby prompting Scout to get off the bed to come and investigate—would be what he should do. Often, avoiding a confrontation is far more effective than going head-to-head with an already headstrong dog.

I told Sam to put Scout's leash on (inside the house) and hold on to it. Sam was to drop something on the floor within eyeshot of the dog, and when Scout went to look at it, Sam was to give a gentle, but firm, correction with the leash and say "leave it." This was to be repeated several times. When the dog began to respect the "correction," Sam was to say "good, leave it," and when Scout sidestepped the item altogether, Sam was to again say "good, leave it" and affectionately pet Scout for his success in following the directive. Practicing this would help the dog to quickly learn that "leave it" meant to not touch it—whatever it was. This "leave it" command would come in handy whenever Scout would begin to bite his own leash or, for that matter, anything else.

I also suggested that Sam begin to use a "gentle leader" or head halter. Like Meghan and her dog, Simon, in chapter 5, Sam could gently but appropriately teach Scout how to walk on the street without incident. This halter is also effective indoors for jumping and a slew of other undesirable behaviors. I didn't think it was a good idea for Scout to leave the house with a toy in his mouth, as it just gave him a reason to guard it and be testy with other dogs on the street. As for Scout's nipping at Sam's hands and whining while he got ready to go to work, that was to be ignored. If Sam did not respond, either negatively or positively, eventually this behavior would just go away. We hoped.

I am relieved to say that Scout's behavior did on the whole, improve. He and Sam have reached a suitable agreement. Sam is the boss and Scout the worker. Sam does miss sleeping with his dog but admits that not cuddling like spoons at night was a fair tradeoff for not being growled at by day. Sam also reported that Scout seemed more relaxed about everything these days. "It was as if," Sam said, "once I became the leader of his pack, he seemed relieved of all need to challenge me.

Amazingly, he actually enjoys doing what I tell him. I'd swear if he could talk he would have explained this 'pack' thing to me from the get-go and I might not have muddled things in the first place."

Sam and Scout are just one of many example of man/dog harmony at its best. Trainers and behaviorists can only hope to achieve this kind of success with just simple behavioral-modification techniques. It must first, however, be understood that not only the dog's behavior needs to be modified.

Admittedly, not all poorly behaved dogs are that way because of their overindulgent companions. Genetics plays a lead role in a dog's behavior, and the blame should not fall on the caretaker too quickly. But, if Fido's mom and dad were upstanding citizens and you have explored (with the help of your veterinarian) the fact that there are no physical reasons for your dog's ugly attitude, then you are free to face the possibility that you just might be living with a brat.

Determining when a nuisance behavior might have begun can often be the clearest way of eliminating it, or at least understanding it. But understanding it and remedying it are two very different things. Although they work hand in hand, finding the emotional chutzpah needed to enforce boundaries seems to be too great a task for many modern dog owners.

Just understanding where you've gone wrong and knowing how to fix it is not enough. One must never forget that condoning brat behavior only encourages these dogs to become repeat offenders. It is our responsibility as their caretakers to teach good manners, putting guilt aside. Well-behaved dogs rarely get reprimanded. Life as a whole for these dogs is far better.

With so much information (new and old) coming from trainers, breeders, dog walkers, animal behaviorists, friends, and family, as well as well-meaning strangers on the street, one might quickly feel oneself reeling in antidotes. Eliminating misbehavior is easiest when done in a three-step program:

Step One: *Keep it simple.* Separate each behavior and treat it as an entity unto itself. Changing one personality trait at a time is far easier than changing an entire personality. Keeping it simple is always better lest you become frustrated by the size of the task and throw in the towel altogether.

Step Two: *No talking.* After the initial reprimand (or warning), stop talking. Conversation only dilutes the clarity of your message. Simply help the dog carry out your wish—after all, you are the teacher.

Step Three: *No emotion.* Emotion usually undermines the end result. If you allow your emotions to interfere when disciplining your dog, you will either go too far or not far enough. Setting the limits well before emotion even comes into the equation will help everyone stay calm.

Once you have determined which specific behavior to modify, complete steps two and three and go about your business. While following these three steps you might be pleasantly surprised to find that your dog is actually more relaxed without all the hoopla usually attached to his repertoire. Your response to a given behavior, desirable or not, is sometimes enough of a reason for that behavior to return.

Like children, dogs who are never required to "think first" are usually out of control and constantly preoccupied with self-need. They will go pretty far to get what they think they need, even snap at "the hand that feeds." Unless you are prepared to continually serve these needs (regardless of the dog's behavior), don't cultivate them in the first place. Teaching and enforcing group respect is a natural part of a dog's thinking process and has been for centuries—why change it now?

Not too long ago I had a client named Jay with a German shepherd named Savannah. Savannah was reasonably well behaved on all counts, as we had worked together when she was only a pup. We hadn't spoken in quite a while, then one evening Jay called to ask my advice about a problem that had developed with Savannah, now ten months old.

The dog, he explained, had a fetish for quilts and had already chewed up four and was well on her way to obliterating the fifth. As Jay could apparently well afford to replace the quilts, he did so each time Savannah destroyed one. I asked him to describe exactly what took place while the dog was "murdering" a quilt and then asked exactly what he did as he witnessed "the murder."

Jay was proud to tell me that whenever he saw Savannah on his bed chewing the quilt, he would quickly scold her and say "off." This usually didn't prompt any response from the dog, so Jay said he then took a step toward her. This made her, almost always (sometimes he had to take two steps closer), jump off the bed and run into her crate. There she would stay and almost cower in shame until Jay (who, by that time, felt bad for having scolded the dog) reached into the crate and rubbed Savannah's belly until she crawled out, only to jump back on the bed and resume chewing on the quilt. I don't get it, he said. She's so smart about every-thing else, you would think she would know by now that chewing the quilt does not make me happy.

I explained that he was, albeit unintentionally, reinforcing the inappropriate behavior by ultimately rewarding the dog in the form of a belly rub. The initial reprimand might have been enough to drive Savannah from the bed, but it was well worth enduring if, at the end of the rainbow, there was a belly rub. If Jay had simply stopped himself from adding emotion to the equation, the dog would more than likely have ceased committing the crimes after quilt number one.

After a moment of silence, during which I was sure Jay was ponder-ing his blunder (having recognized what all this must have meant to the dog), I felt certain that this brat behavior was soon to be a thing of the past. His response, however, was not at all what I had expected. He explained that confusing or upsetting his dog was never his intention and, rather than fix the problem (which required reprimanding the dog), he would much rather condone it. Now Savannah just chews the quilt while Jay rubs her belly. Case closed.

Choosing what seems to be the path of least resistance when living with a dog often leads to the longest and bumpiest road. If you indulge a dog, even for a brief period (whether it is to service your own needs or the dog's), you will eventually tire of playing servant. When you do, your dog will most assuredly act out and, when that happens, the dynamics of your entire relationship will change. You then begin the downward spiral of contests between you and the dog, leaving you little else to cling to but a few rose-colored ideas of what you thought life with a dog would be like.

When this happens, be careful not to go to extremes. One should never consider catering to another creature's every whim and then slapping him in the face for expecting to be catered to. Try a reasonable alternative first. Slowly changing your behavior will alert the dog that change is in the air. If his usual antics no longer prompt your usual response, he will naturally try another tack. If this new behavior pleases you, reward it and the dog will then repeat that behavior. Not only that, the dog will consider it an honor to have been included in the "workings" of the pack.

Dogs take great pride in the roles they play within their own immediate social circles. These roles actually measure a dog's feeling of self-worth and are necessary for overall survival. If you don't give dogs anything to do, they eventually feel worthless. This only leaves a dog searching for a purpose; unfortunately, that purpose often becomes pushing you (and everyone else they come in contact with) around.

One woman, who was not a client but an acquaintance, had a dog (a papillon) who was a brat dog if ever there was one. This dog had been spoiled so rotten that I believe he had actually forgotten he was a dog. He urinated (indoors) wherever he wished and no sooner had he done it than someone was there to clean it up. His wardrobe was extensive and his owner swore that he "strutted" when he wore his handmade, Harley-Davidson leather jacket. He was, of course, short on patience with just about everyone he came in contact with. He ate only fresh, steamed fish and, if it wasn't just the right temperature when served, he wouldn't eat at all.

He did, however, tolerate the woman. It seems she never required anything from him so she never suffered his wrath. They lived alone, as a pack of two, and with the exception of the woman's staff (who were paid to be servants) had little reason to tolerate the masses of the outside world. A friend of the woman's once suggested she send him to boarding school where he might learn some real manners. She thought the idea preposterous but has nonetheless taken to repeating the anecdote at parties—one of which I happened to attend.

Foolishly and egotistically, I attempted to right the woman's perspective by explaining that her dog might be happier if she would make a few painless adjustments in the dog's daily routine. She took polite offense to my thinking that I could possibly know what was best for her precious pup, then admitted that she simply could not and would not change how she lived with this dog. I thanked her for her candor and wished her good luck.

The dog's original role is that of a hard worker. The latchkey dog has learned to become a hard player. Believe it or not, dogs enjoy nothing more than a good, thought-provoking challenge—even if that challenge is you. I fear, if we continue to elevate our dogs to the status of demigod, they will simply have less patience for us peasants.

Chapter 7

Cagey Situations

To Crate or Not to Crate

Cages—everybody's talking about them. In fact, cages, or crates, have become the subject of great debate. Are they training tools or training tools or training traps? Are they cruel or kind? Do they benefit our dogs or us? Is time spent in a cage simply time spent in a cage or is it a temporary reprieve from the stress of daily life? Well, it all depends on how you look at it. But, if you look at it as a modern dog would, you'd probably view a crate as the one sacred shrine you have left—one that pays homage to your ancestry and represents the only constant fixture in your life.

Cages have been around for roughly as long as the domesticated dog. A small, enclosed space, they replicate the safe den of long ago. While most dogs seem pretty pleased about crates, it is their human owners who bring extremely mixed feelings to the subject.

For transportation purposes, cages were employed to keep traveling most dogs safe. For containment purposes, cages were a convenience as well as a boundary. For training purposes, cages were a means of control. Regardless of the crate's long history as a positive tool, countless numbers of modern dog-loving people are having a hard time caging, or "crating," their dogs.

Now, it's fairly understandable that the image of an animal locked up in a tiny space would probably make anyone uncomfortable. That is, any human. But, what if the idea of being confined to a small space didn't make you uncomfortable at all but, rather, made you feel secure and safe? Dogs, believe it or not, instinctively seek out tight spaces with low ceilings to soothe themselves as well as to diminish the amount of territory they feel the need to protect.

When female dogs are about to give birth, they search for small, sheltered areas—areas with at least two opaque sides—as the safest places to bear their young. When dogs are not well, they are not comfortable in wide-open spaces but, instead, seek the shelter of dimly lit, covered spaces. Doing so makes them feel less exposed to outside dangers and, at the very least, out of harm's way. Some dogs will even dig a deep hole to die in, sensing their vulnerability when death is near. Young pups will instinctively avoid venturing far from the safety of the den (a cavelike dwelling with only one common entry and exit). Historically, large spaces with wide-open skies left them unprotected from predators. Practically then, it seems the great crating debate is best settled by the dogs themselves. Because dogs have the innate need to patrol and protect any territory that they consider their own, the less space a dog has to worry about, the better. Believe it or not, that wide-open space needn't be a sprawling field—it might just be your house.

When used properly, a crate should be viewed as a safe harbor or a pseudo den rather than as a cage or a jail cell. Access to a crate saves many dogs the unnecessary stress of wandering the house all day looking for a dark, tight space in which to rest their bones. Dogs who have the luxury of their own crates are often spared the trauma of many behavioral dilemmas that develop as a result of the dog not having a place of its own. Many dogs resort to creating their own dens: under coffee tables or piano benches or even under our beds. But whether you supply the building materials or they do their own house hunting, the point is: From puppyhood to old age, every dog needs a den.

The dog crate, when used properly, offers a solution to the many day-to-day dilemmas facing the modern dog. Not only can it prove helpful when raising and housebreaking a puppy, but it is even more valuable for the dog who spends a good deal of its daylight hours alone. Furthermore, the dog whose immediate social circle has been extended to include the walker, the groomer, the day care staff, and the weekend sitter can benefit from the constancy of a crate. A crate, especially to latchkey dogs, represents a necessary constant in an otherwise inconsistent world.

Housebreaking is just one of the many uses for a crate. When introducing a new dog to existing family pets, temporarily isolating the new dog in a crate helps to ease household tension—for the old as well as the new. The crate simply functions as a barrier that prevents unwanted incidents. More often than not, a crate can help to make the difference in the overall well-being of a puppy embarking on a new life with a new family.

Because raising puppies can sometimes try men's souls, the decision of whether or not to use a crate often becomes the pivotal factor in the success or failure of your relationship with this youngster. It not only helps to separate the two of you when you both need a little downtime, but it also helps you to keep the dog safe from the many dangers around the house—exposed wires, valuable property, exposed flesh, and a surplus of "chokables" left out in the open. It also helps to begin the housebreaking process and, without it, many of us are left to battle a "sharp-toothed" tiger running about looking for a place to rest as well as to eliminate.

Ideally, a puppy begins life jammed into a small space shared by its mother and siblings. The pack eats together (side by side), plays together (with body parts entwined), and sleeps together (bunched into neat little piles to retain warmth). So, whether locked mouth to mouth in play, sleeping triple decker, or fighting for the best spot in the cafeteria, right from the start, close is the theme. The moment a puppy strays from the group, the mother dog herds it back into the safety of the fold. This cultivates a dog's natural desire to be in secure, tight spaces just as it reinforces the pack mentality: *Stay close and stay together.*

When a puppy makes the transition from canine family to human family, his need to be close does not wane, and should be considered a priority. Because the dog's human family cannot possibly spend twenty-four hours a day snuggled up with or supervising the dog, it is critical that we recognize the need to provide the dog with some security in our absence. Which brings us to the crate. When sized properly for the individual dog (enough space to stand up with its head extended, and with the room to turn a full circle, lie down, and stretch out), the crate becomes the perfect transitional space between whelping box and big house. Even a small apartment is a big space to a young pup. If you live in a large house, to a puppy it's a veritable continent. Each room represents another country to navigate and, if you don't know your way around, navigation can be a daunting undertaking. Even leaving the puppy gated in the confines of a bathroom or a kitchen can be more than a puppy can handle. Since the average ceiling is at least eight feet high, any room can seem a virtual gymnasium to a dog looking for a low roof under which to shelter its body. Providing a space that re-creates a natural cavelike dwelling (especially when covered by a towel or a sheet on the top and three of its sides) offers your dog familiar shelter as well as peace of mind.

Pup Tents

About a year ago, I worked with a family that had an eleven-month-old keeshond named Jeffrey. At almost a year of age, Jeffrey was still not yet reliably housebroken. He had chewed almost everything of value in the house and dug up everything of value outside the house. Because misery often seeks company, Jeffrey's family decided to contact the family who had adopted one of Jeffrey's brothers. They did so in the hope of discussing what they assumed would be a common problem—after all, same dog family, same dog behavior . . . right? What they discovered was eye-opening, to say the least. Jeffrey's littermate, Teddy, didn't share his brother's problem at all. In fact, as Teddy's family rattled off their dog's accomplishments, one after another, Jeffrey's family decided that Jeffrey must simply be a "lemon."

After comparing the details of how each pup had been raised after being adopted by their respective human families (at the age of seven weeks), it became clear that the only significant difference between Jeffrey and Teddy's daily life was that Teddy's routine included the use of a crate. As Jeffrey's family was strongly averse to "locking up" any dog, least of all their own, Jeffrey's had not.

Teddy's family boasted that their dog had been housebroken "in no time" and, since he had been safely ensconced in his crate whenever they left the house or could not supervise his activity, Teddy had done no material damage to their property. Whenever they were at home, Teddy was released from the crate and busy learning (with supervised help) what he could and could not do with his freedom. As a result, at eleven months of age, Teddy had free run of the house and slept (happily) in the crate at night or whenever the family was not at home. Teddy's family had the peace of mind of knowing that when they were not around, their young dog was safe in his "den."

As for Jeffrey, it was becoming rapidly apparent that his freedom had actually been the cause of his difficulties. Because he was never confined to a resting space that he would instinctively want to keep clean, he would simply eliminate in one space and rest in another—some distance away from "the mess."

Because he had little or no supervision on his jaunts around the house, modifying Jeffrey's behavior became impossible. The result of this was that Jeffrey often mistook his family's belongings for chew toys. The digging outdoors was more than likely a result of his having too much "open sky" to deal with; with his innate need to find shelter, Jeffrey was merely attempting to build a shelter of his own.

After weighing the facts, Jeffrey's family wholeheartedly agreed that the stand they had taken against crating had probably cost them a blissful first year with their puppy and, if they had it to do over again, they would undoubtedly use a crate.

When trying to come to terms with whether or not to crate a puppy, a person can unwittingly send messages of doubt to the puppy itself, thus making the actual exercise of crating even more of a challenge than usual. If you decide to give it a try, remember, crating is good for the dog; your ambivalent feelings about the matter will only serve to muddy the waters. Try to find some solace in knowing at least this: Whenever you don't know where your puppy is, he is more than likely up to no good, so the crate is actually the next best thing to being in your arms.

Also remember that the more you supervise, the more time the pup can and should be out of the crate learning how to behave properly in his new surroundings. The crate functions as a safety net for the puppy when you are not in a position to supervise his activities. To you, closing a crate door means your puppy can't get out. To the puppy, it means nothing spooky or threatening can get in.

Because individual personalities dictate different needs, some puppies have a greater desire to be close to their pack members than they do to find shelter, so crate socializing your puppy first is a step well worth taking. Here's how.

Choosing a Crate

Before discussing how to acclimate a dog or a puppy to a crate, let's take a moment to discuss which kind of crate to purchase. Although some would disagree, I strongly recommend the wire, collapsible kind. They break down to a near-flat surface for transport and they also allow ventilation better than do the plastic or fiberglass travel kennels. The wire crate offers you the option to cover as much or as little of the dog's line of vision to outside stimuli as you desire. If your dog prefers to have only the top covered, you can easily leave the sides uncovered, or if the opening or door of your dog's crate faces a different direction than you would like the dog to face, rather than drag or shift the crate to another location, you may simply tip up the sheet or towel and expose the side you want the dog to see out of.

Now let's talk about what size crate you need. A dog must have *at least* enough room to stand up (head extended), turn around, lie down, and stretch out in, but a puppy should (in the infant stage) have only that much room; otherwise it might nest or sleep in one portion of the crate and use another portion as a toilet. A too large crate also deprives the puppy of feeling it has something to snuggle up against. When sizing a crate, purchase one that will accommodate your dog's adult size—puppies grow at a breakneck speed and (depending on your breed), your five-pound, seven-week-old pup will be thirty pounds in just a few short weeks, so bigger (in the crate department) is always better. You can, and often must, modify the crate to fit your infant dog (by inserting a cage divider), then extend its size as the puppy grows. If your puppy learns quickly and has a proven record of keeping the crate clean, give him more space. That said, let's talk about how to crate.

After you have chosen the crate that best suits you and your dog's lifestyle, set it up before you get the puppy/dog (assuming you have this luxury) and, if you have children, let them play in it to their heart's content. After the puppy comes, the crate should belong to him only, so letting the kids use it until it is no longer a novelty often eliminates a struggle later on. Place the crate in a low-traffic area and don't forget to cover it, leaving the best vantage point facing out. Without the cover or makeshift ceiling, it is not a den, but is instead just a cage in the middle of a room. Let the puppy find his own way inside and set it up like a cozy bedroom so he feels at home once inside.

Crate Socializing

Crate socializing does not take a preset amount of time—each puppy is different. Many pet shop puppies (who have been in a cage for an extended period of time) might have a negative association with the crate. Be patient and practice the following steps and even the most resistant youngster should come around.

• **Make the experience pleasant.** If you begin the introduction process by always leaving a small treat at the back of the crate, the puppy will associate entering the crate with a food reward and puppy and crate will become fast friends.

• **Don't shut and lock the door right away.** Let the puppy wander in and out several times until he feels the lay of the land, praising him softly whenever he does go in. When you do begin to shut the door, do this for only a moment at a time, opening and shutting the door often enough that the puppy does not associate the closed door with being separated from you. Each time he comes out, put another treat in the crate. Eventually, the puppy will go in for the treat and wait for you to praise him.

• **Keep dialogue to a minimum.** The more talking you do, the more likely you are to send the wrong message with the tone of your voice. For example, if the puppy instantly starts crying when you shut the crate door, you might just soothingly tell him that everything is okay or even open the door. He will more than likely interpret his crying as a behavior that pleases you (given your soothing tone or the open door) and will then repeat the behavior whenever you close the crate door. Thus, you end up with a puppy that has actually been trained to cry at even the prospect of a closed crate door. Instead, whenever you are closing and opening the door (with the puppy in the crate), make the exercise as benign as possible. Ignore crying, within reason. Most youngsters will soon realize that the door that shuts also opens.

• **Always praise the pup for going in.** Whether it's by command or choice, always let your dog know that his going "in" to his own place pleases you and say nothing at all when he is coming out.

• **Do *not*, under any circumstance, use the crate for punishment.** The crate is the place the dog should always be able to rely on when it needs to feel safe. If you use the crate for any negative reason, the puppy or dog will begin to fear what should otherwise be a comfort station.

• **Make the crate a friendly zone.** Keep it comfortable with non-chokeable toys and perhaps a T-shirt that has been worn by one or all family members. The more user-friendly you make it, the more inviting it is to the dog.

• **Crates make ideal bedrooms.**   Place the crate as close to your sleeping area as possible—dogs feel more secure when the pack sleeps together. Whether you keep the door closed for a puppy or open for a mature dog, your dog will enjoy having a room of his own.

• **Limit the time spent in the crate.**   Dogs do not learn how you expect them to behave "out" of the crate if they are always in the crate. Never leave a puppy in the crate for more than three hours or an adult dog for more than four to five.

Housebreaking

Once your puppy begins to trust that the crate is a friendly zone and has found himself a comfortable place within its walls, begin the house-breaking (or paper-training) process immediately.

When using your crate as a housebreaking tool, the idea is to help to strengthen the puppy's new muscles until they are strong enough to stay tight, even when the puppy is wandering around a larger space, such as your house. Remember, if the crate space is too big, the puppy will rest in one part and eliminate in another. When the puppy learns that your house is not a toilet (and he eventually does this by your telling him this), he will wait, by using his newly strengthened muscles, until you take him to the place where he has been taught that he can eliminate.

I strongly recommend taking your puppy on-leash (even those who have large, fenced-in yards) each time to a specific bathroom spot. Other-wise, the puppy might think it is okay to use your entire yard as a toilet, which is neither wise nor sanitary. When the puppy is on-leash, you are there to supervise and praise appropriate behavior. But if you just let him "out" on his own, you might assume that he has sufficiently emp-tied his bladder and bowels only to find a mess on the floor shortly after you let him back in the house.

In the beginning (the infant stage of seven to twelve weeks), some puppies cannot and will not even try to hold their bladder and bowels.

With the strong need to eliminate, or a large enough space to eliminate and step out of the way, accidents are bound to happen. Do not, however, despair. Accidents are, believe it or not, a necessary part of the process—as long as you are there to teach him not to do it again.

- **Keep housebreaking as simple a task as possible.** Remember, everything is new to a puppy, so be a patient parent and an even more patient teacher. The puppy's infant stage is the shortest of all and, if you use your time wisely, he will be a trustworthy member of the family in no time at all.

- **Set up a fair schedule.** Keep in mind that a puppy has to go to the bathroom several times a day. The rule of thumb is, no longer than five to fifteen minutes after each time his belly is full (whether it is with water, food, or treats) and no longer than five to fifteen minutes into any kind of physical activity. He can hold his bladder and bowels considerably longer when he is resting or sleeping (sometimes as long as eight hours), but each puppy has its own capacity.

- **Keep a housebreaking schedule taped to the refrigerator.** On it, record the day and each time you take the puppy to the designated toilet. Note also what he did while he was there. Also, record accidents—what time they occurred and where they were. Within three or four days, you should have a pretty good idea of how many times a day, and when, your youngster needs to move his bowels (counting accidents) and at least a fair estimate (counting accidents) of how many times he needs to pee and approximately how long he can hold his bladder when resting or playing. Don't be alarmed if your puppy empties his bladder even more than a dozen times a day or moves his bowels four to six times in a twenty-four-hour period. Young muscles have little control, but control will come in time.

- **Crate him only when his bladder and bowels are empty.** Keeping in mind that puppies have young, inexperienced muscles and that accidents do happen, make certain to not put your puppy in a crate unless his bladder and bowels are empty and, again, never leave your puppy crated for more than three hours at a time.

• **Keep the crate door closed at night.** Nighttime is the only time to crate a puppy for more than the three-hour limit. Be sure that your youngster's bladder and bowels are empty before a long stay in the crate. Place the crate next to or close to your bed. Puppies almost always need to feel close to their people during the night. Shut the door, even if he whines a little. This will teach him to control and strengthen his bladder and bowel muscles.

• **Always bring the puppy to a "bathroom spot" whenever and as soon as you take him out of the crate.** Puppies spend most of their crate time resting and (as any parent will tell you) when a baby wakes up, that baby always has to pee. Better to be safe than sorry, so set the puppy up for success (going to the bathroom in a place of your choice) rather than failure (an accident on the floor).

• **Stay calm whenever you are taking the puppy out of the crate.** If you get too excited (with your greeting) while you are taking him out, he will only "pee in his pants" and soil himself, all of his hard work to hold it in (while he was crated) will have been for naught. Because healthy puppies are instinctively clean creatures, keeping their own crate free of waste becomes a natural priority. Without the mother dog to clean up after her pups, the pup learns to hold his bladder and bowels until he can eliminate in an area some distance from his sleeping quarters, and his sleeping quarters, in this case, should be the crate.

• **Never assume a puppy does *not* have to go to the bathroom.** If your youngster is having trouble making the transition from paper to street, don't assume he does not have to "go" if he doesn't eliminate outside. Your pup always has to go but he might just be waiting until he is inside (on the paper), where you initially taught him he *should* eliminate. Give him a chance in the newly chosen outdoor spot and if he is not successful, take him inside, crate him for no longer than five minutes, then, take him back out again. If you bring him inside and put him down (because you assume he must not have to go to the bathroom), he will immediately soil in the old, acceptable spot because he thinks it is still an acceptable spot. If you are lucky enough to witness such a mistake, scold the puppy (sharply enough to stop him in the middle of the act) and bring him immediately to the outside spot to finish, praising him if he does. If he doesn't finish, crate him for five-minute intervals, trying again until he is successful.

• **Look forward to the accidents you are fortunate enough to witness.** Without them, a puppy never learns where he should not go to the bathroom.

• **Only modify behavior that you actually witness.** Dogs, for the most part, think in the present tense, so don't waste your time or damage your puppy's tender psyche (or an adult dog's, for that matter) by reprimanding him for something you did not actually see happening. If you punish behavior that you did not witness, the only thing it will teach your dog is to be afraid of you. On the other hand, if you are careful to catch mistakes "in progress" and never punish for something that has been done in your absence, you will soon stop your dog from repeating the offense.

Once your puppy is reliably housebroken, the only thing that changes about the crate is the status of the door—simply leave it open and let the dog decide when he needs it.

Some dogs need their crate well beyond puppyhood. Reaching the adult stage does not automatically exempt a dog from needing a den. In fact, for some dogs it's quite the opposite.

Many modern dogs have begun to present us with dog-rearing issues that a century ago would have seemed outrageous. What to do with the dog during the day (while you were gone) was never a topic for discussion because someone was always home. These days, however, the dog is often the only family member at home. Obviously, all this solitude has an effect on our dogs. Some seem to adapt well, but those who don't are communicating their problems quite clearly. Separation anxiety, obsessive-compulsive barking, and physically destructive behavior are just some expressions of the problems plaguing our latchkey dogs.

Because dogs are naturally codependent creatures, the physical presence of the pack functions as a main ingredient in a dog's well-being. When the pack is not around, the dog feels himself to be responsible for the property in which the pack dwells. This leaves the dog vulnerable to a great deal of stress. Outside noises that would not bother a dog in the company of his pack become "threatening intruders" for the solitary dog. Whether the sounds are simply traffic on the street or a neighbor pulling into his own driveway, a dog (without a signal from a pack member) cannot differentiate which intruders to ignore and so stresses about all of them.

Because the survival of the dog pack depends on a complex set of social rules through which the dogs protect each other and their territory as a team, protecting the domain of the human pack (the house) is frequently too big a job for one pack member to handle. Decreasing a dog's protective instinct can be nearly impossible. Decreasing the amount of space a dog feels he must protect, however, is possible. Therefore, lessening the size of a dog's living space would seem like the best solution. For overly protective or anxious dogs, a crate is just what the doctor ordered.

Dog-Den Afternoons . . .

Barney was a shelter dog who was adopted by Kurt and Amy when he was about seven months old. Initially crate trained, once he was reliably housebroken he was allowed the run of the house. Barney was very intelligent, which made obedience training a snap. The more Kurt and Amy gave their dog to think about, the better. For two years Barney lived with his people and all was right with the world. Then Amy decided to take a job, which meant Barney would have to spend the better part of the weekdays alone. Amy and Kurt installed a dog door so Barney could go outside whenever he wanted to and, of course, gave him total freedom throughout the house. About two months after Amy went back to work, she and Kurt noticed that a corner had been chewed off of one of the couch pillows. The two thought little of it until they came home to find the quilt from their bed shredded all over the house. A few days later they saw that one of the floorboards by the front door had been scratched beyond repair. They checked Barney's front paws and found them badly bloodied. Worried, they called their veterinarian for advice.

Their vet told them that Barney might be having a hard time with Amy's no longer being home during the day and that they might want to try crating him during their absence. *Crating him!* "How," Kurt and Amy thought, "could putting their dog in a cage possibly make him feel better?"

What ailed Barney was not simply the fact that Amy was no longer at home but, moreover, that with Amy no longer at home, he was left to guard the house all by himself. He had been used to taking cues from her whenever a visitor came to call or a sound echoed outside the walls of their lair. If she didn't seem concerned, neither did he. But, without her there to remind him that the responsibility of taking care of the house was hers and not his, he felt totally responsible for protecting it, at least until Amy and Kurt got home. That instantly turned noises that Barney otherwise slept through into warning sirens that someone might be intruding on his family's space. Even the telephone startled him now. He had, without a doubt, been transformed from a calm, cool, and collected canine into a nail-biting wreck.

Thankfully, Amy and Kurt decided to heed the doctor's advice and got Barney a crate. They set it up in their bedroom because it was the quietest room in the house and left it open for a few days. They covered it, leaving the side facing the bedroom door free from obstruction and filled it with a few of the dog's favorite toys. They even sacrificed the pillow he had begun to chew, thinking it was probably covered with their smell and that this might have been the reason he'd chosen it when he was feeling stressed. They also asked a friend to come over to take Barney for a bathroom break and a short walk in the middle of the day.

They were skeptical, at first, so they set up a video camera in the bedroom to record what actually happened when they were gone. To their pleasant surprise, the result was a dog that slept during most of the day. Whenever he heard a noise inside or outside the house, he raised his head, looked around the crate, sighed, (in a gesture that suggested *everything's cool in here*) and went back to sleep. The couple was amazed and delighted. To be sure that Barney's time in the crate was not counterproductive, Amy and Kurt also made sure that he got plenty of exercise when they were home. They were also surprised to find that at night Barney went into the crate on his own. He actually preferred sleeping in his crate to sleeping in bed with them. Cagey, no—comforting, yes!

Dogs will do whatever it takes to please their people, but sometimes the species gap throws us a curveball that prevents people from understanding what it takes to please their dog. The results can sometimes be disastrous. If more people were open to crating their dogs—in a humane and balanced manner—during their absence, the result would be calmer and more contented dogs.

There are so many reasons why a dog might need a crate and all of these reasons stem from dogs' basic need to stay close and stay together. The theory that lessening the square footage a dog is required to protect if you are not around is an easy enough concept to swallow, but what about the dogs who spend their days being shuffled from activity to activity, or from person to person?

Twice a day with the dog walker and three times a week at day care. Three weekends a month at the country house and one weekend with the dog-sitter. Dogs who have what I call "extended packs" (dogs who live with their immediate pack but spend a good deal of time with other people, or outside pack members) are the quintessential latchkey dogs and they need a crate more than you could imagine. This dog has a hard enough time just keeping track of its own family. With little in its life that remains constant, the crate represents a familiar resting place as well as a home away from home. Giving this dog a crate would be like soothing the savage beast.

Don't Leave Home Without It

I first met Cruise, a three-year-old rottweiler, at a regional dog show. He was one of the most well-trained dogs I had ever seen and his handsome stature drew instant attention. He had an expression in his eyes that reminded me of a dog I'd had as a child that was very close to my heart. I was immediately drawn to him. I was surprised when his owner/breeder told me that he was actually for sale. Tempting though it was, at the time I was not in a position to purchase the dog. I commented, however, that whoever ended up with this dog would be fortunate to inherit such a well-trained beast.

About two years later I received a message on my answering machine from someone inquiring about my training services. The young man on the message mentioned that his dog, Cruise, was giving him quite a hard time and he was in search of a trainer. For an instant, I allowed myself to think this might be the same Cruise I had seen at the dog show two years earlier. It seemed impossible, not only because I had not mentioned to the breeder that I was a trainer, but because the Cruise I had met, however briefly, was definitely not in need of training. Anyway, I figured there was more than one dog in the world named Cruise and, on that note, I returned the call.

As fate would have it, it was indeed the same rottweiler I had met two years earlier, and to my surprise, the dog this man described sounded like a real mess.

The young man, Steven, explained that he had purchased Cruise two years earlier and the experience had been a nightmare since day one. To begin with, the dog had originally moved in with Steven and his girlfriend. Steven was soon called out of town on business, so he left Cruise with his girlfriend. About two months later, the girlfriend found another boyfriend and this left Cruise in the middle of a pack war. Steven (devastated about losing his girlfriend but more devastated about the prospect of "some stranger" raising Cruise) flew home and promptly moved out of his girlfriend's apartment, dog and all. Because he was not yet finished with his out-of-town business, Cruise stayed with several friends over the course of the next six months. By the time Steven returned, Cruise was no longer the well-trained, handsome dog that Steven had originally purchased. Although he was certain that the dog was properly cared for, it was apparent that Cruise had not only lost weight but had also lost the light in his eyes. Upset by what he saw, Steven concluded his out-of-town business, rented a studio apartment, and set up a "proper" home for his dog.

As Steven was required to be at the office most of the day, hiring a dog-walking service was the first order of business. He opted for a "pack walk" (dogs walking in groups), thinking Cruise might like to spend more time with other dogs. Determined to "do it right" this time around, Steven found a wonderful day care facility that also offered dog-sitting services if he absolutely had to go out of town. Cruise went out with a walker twice a day, spent one day a week at day care, and spent an average of two nights a month at their overnight facility. Everything was now right with the world . . . or was it?

Instead of improving, Cruise's health was rapidly deteriorating, as was his behavior. He no longer followed even the simple obedience commands that had once been as easy for this dog as breathing. And, as if things could get any worse, Steven received a call from one of the dog walkers explaining that Cruise no longer wanted to go for his walks. Getting him to go outside had become more like a game of tug-of-war. Steven called his vet for advice and he suggested that he call me.

By the time I arrived on the scene, Cruise was a mere shadow of the dog I had met just two short years earlier. I was astonished! Although he was still a young and vital five-year-old dog, he seemed frighteningly near death's door. After discussing the situation with Steven, the first thing that seemed abundantly clear was that there was very little constancy in this dog's life. I questioned Steven about whether or not Cruise had a crate and he explained that, although the breeder had given him one when he got the dog, space being limited, he—not thinking it was necessary—had just stored it away.

After explaining the significance of the crate as a den, especially for a dog that had spent his early years using one (at the breeder's), and stressing the importance of a constant in a dog's life, we immediately got the crate out of storage and proceeded to set it up in what little space was left in the apartment.

Knowing full well that supplying this dog with a crate would not simply and miraculously cure him of all that ailed him, I suggested that Steven change Cruise's walks from pack walks to individual walks and with the same walker each day. This would eliminate at least one pack that Cruise felt the need to find his place within and would require him to adjust to only one new face coming to pick him up at home each day.

Another necessary prescription would be to make sure that wherever this dog went for more than a few hours, whether it was a weekend away with Steven or an overnight at day care, his crate was absolutely and without question to go with him. Last, but not at all the least important of my instructions, was for Steven to reteach Cruise his obedience commands. This would give him a clear sense of who was in charge and would help to solidify his relationship with Steven. Allowing the dog to rely on the man's leadership would almost act as a sedative for his pack instability. Cruise was a dog without a reliable pack and he needed one badly.

Having to adjust to yet another life change, Cruise was, to say the least, a bit skeptical at first. He continued to resist going for walks until he got used to seeing the same walker each day. Once he began to trust this person as a reliable extended pack member, he began to look forward to the daily outings. Not having to prove himself with the other dogs, as he had on his old pack walks, sped up the healing process considerably.

He did, however, take to the crate almost immediately. Just seeing it again must have been like seeing an old friend. After an hour or so of smelling his way around it (making certain it was, in fact, his crate), Cruise set up shop as if he was "home." Now, when he is not out with his walker, at day care, or busy following Steven's lead, he is comfortably resting in his crate. And, whenever he spends a night away from home, wherever that might be, his old friend (the crate) always goes with him.

Although Cruise's situation is clearly extreme, there are, in fact, many modern dogs whose families break up, leaving them to deal with upheaval and with little to rely on. Whatever the reason (i.e., divorce, breakup, grown children moving out), these dogs would benefit from, at the very least, a room of their own. Nonetheless, a dog does not have to change families and surroundings a half dozen times within the first two years of its life in order to suffer the burden of being cageless.

With alternatives such as dog walkers and day care facilities available to the modern dog owner, there is little reason to keep your dog isolated within the confines of your home just because you can't be there to do the walking or the playing. In fact, with so many options to choose from, it has actually become easier to overdo rather than leave undone.

As a responsible leader of your dog's pack, knowing how the world looks from the dog's perspective simply serves to assist you in setting up the healthiest routine possible.

Crates are not the answer for all dogs, but supplying one functions as a preventive measure for a slew of behavioral problems that just might creep up and bite you from behind later on. Don't assume that because your dog no longer needs a crate for training purposes that he no longer needs it for peace of mind. When your puppy is reliably housebroken and teething is a stage that you recall only dimly, just leave the crate door open and allow the dog to use it when he feels the need. If you think your dog is one of those secure canines that feels grounded wherever he goes and you are tired of looking at the homemade, shanty-town decor of the cage, try redesigning it rather than relinquishing it. But remember, be careful never to abuse the privilege of the crate. It is there to encourage serenity, not to baby-sit, and under no circumstance is it there for punishment. Leaving a dog confined for extended periods of time only opens the great dog-crate debate to well-founded skepticism, leaving many dogs searching for a place to hide rather than a place to rest.

Monitor your dog's time spent in the crate and keep an eye on when and why you think he is using it. Extremes, in all cases, are not healthy, so even the dog who is, by its own choice, spending an excessive amount of time in its crate should give rise to concern. Heed the few simple rules of crate socializing and crate training (mentioned earlier in this chapter) and the crate might just turn out to be the best friend you (and your dog) ever had.

Dogs do not mind a change of scenery, as long as the pack remains the same. In a modern world, unfortunately, the pack no longer stays down on the farm and the dog, in many cases, has been left to negotiate the day alone. Having something that remains familiar to the dog when it simply cannot be you will help the dog to adjust to any situation. For those of us who travel with our dogs, the crate affords the luxury of a security blanket in a strange place.

So, as the modern dog owner continues his quest for ever increasing ways to enrich the life of his millennium mutt, and as we search the Internet for new ways to fill our dog's days with stimulating activities and thought-provoking toys, shouldn't we give at least a thought to the importance of providing a resting place that mimics the dog's natural, age-old dwelling? In fact, shouldn't this be at the very top of the list?

Of course, the great dog-crate debate will continue as long as dog owners let their own feelings—rather than reason—rule. But, for those who are still on the fence about whether crating a dog might be "bad," keep in mind that not crating a dog might prove to be far worse.

Chapter 8

Great Expectations

When the Dog's Behavior Runs Away with Your Emotions

Expectations come in all shapes and sizes. When deciding what yours are going to be in your relationship with your dog, keep in mind, the bigger they are, the harder they fall!

After nine weeks (that often seem like nine months) of preparation—reading all the latest literature on "proper technique," learning how to test for high IQ, determining the personality and behavioral traits best suited to your family, and considering at length such issues as appearance and gender—the baby is finally born.

The next step is to rush out and buy all the necessary—and often unnecessary—accessories to set up shop for the new family member. The books explain from A to Z what you are supposed to do—or avoid doing—to make this relationship work. With great expectations you anticipate the tasks before you.

There's no turning back now. You've signed the necessary papers and, except for a few formalities, you're almost home. You review all the instructions in your head and you know you are reasonably and responsibly prepared. But one thing keeps nagging at you. It's been in the back of your mind since the conception of the idea to expand the family. The question is: Once the new family member arrives, will it be everything you expect it to be?

I refer, of course to the addition of a dog (rather than a human child) to a family. But does the species really matter, considering the depth of emotion attached to the experience of child rearing? Being responsible for another life is a pretty big deal and doing it right is a mighty tall order. It's easy to be overwhelmed. Fantasizing about the successes of the relationship and ignoring the potential failures can make even the smallest disappointment seem monumental. The failures are just as important as the successes when it comes to shaping this important relationship.

Loving a dog, once you have decided to share your life with one, begins well before your first meeting. It begins with your private expectations of what the relationship will ultimately be. Whether it is the image of you reading the evening paper by firelight with your dog blissfully curled up at your feet or of your children running with the dog through a field covered by wildflowers, the sun on their skin and smiles on their faces, the expectations exist, and they are not small. And why should they be? If the image you conjured up was one of "Cujo," slobbering all over your sliding glass door as he viciously clawed his way into the house, growling and nipping at the back of your pants, no sane person would ever think of adopting a dog. Our fantasies get us to the plate. The fact that dreamy images and actual reality are not necessarily similar simply means that some of us have some adjusting to do.

Wouldn't it be wonderful if every dog came complete with its own instruction manual to guide you through those emotional rough spots (kind of a training manual for your feelings)? If such a thing existed, we might be more inclined to have a go at living with a dog or, better yet, sticking with the dog we already have. Relationships are never without their ups and downs, and knowing what to do in the middle of a down can be the saving grace of the entire relationship. Even Lassie wasn't a "wonder dog" until she (or, in reality, *he*) was actually trained.

Love Hurts

I answered the phone to the sound of crying. After Lisa, the woman on the other end, calmed down a bit, she explained that she had recently adopted a seven-week-old, mixed-breed puppy for herself and her nine-year-old son, Eric. In the three weeks since they had brought the puppy home, they had successfully taught him to "sit," "down," "stay," walk nicely on a lead, and come when called. (All of this, by the way, is an extraordinary feat for any ten-week-old puppy.) Assuming from this information that the woman's tears must naturally be tears of joy, I remarked that I, too, might cry such grateful tears if I had had the good fortune to work with such an apt pupil. It seemed, however, that these were not tears of joy but were, in fact, tears of emotional frustration.

After months of discussing the pros and cons of adding a dog to their family, Lisa had decided the time was finally right. A dog would be a welcome distraction for a boy growing up without a father and Lisa thought the responsibility of caring for another life would be an enriching experience for both of them to share. "And besides," Lisa added, "it would feel good to have a baby in the house again."

Mother and son chose their dog from a rather large litter of pups that had been brought to their local shelter just days before. They named the pup Luke and brought him home. They were prepared to experience the overwhelming joy of getting a puppy. They were not prepared for the fact that Luke (like every other puppy) came equipped with a standard set of razor-sharp milk teeth. Given this, they were certainly not prepared for the fact that Luke was going to use these teeth every chance he got, and not only on his owner's most precious possessions, but directly on his owners as well. This, apparently and understandably, was why Lisa was in tears. Her otherwise "perfect" dog was literally trying to eat her and her child alive and, after just a few short weeks, they had numerous scars to prove it. It had stirred in Lisa such feelings of exasperation and anger that she had actually contemplated leaving Luke at the shelter door and stealing away in the dead of night. That this was not at all what she had expected went without saying, and she felt totally blindsided by the anger and despair this behavior sparked in her. What Lisa didn't know was that Luke's crocodilian ways were simply an expression of normal, healthy, necessary, developmental puppy behavior.

After explaining the do's and don'ts of teething, I also explained to Lisa that living with a puppy was not always like living with a human child. Some things just had to be considered from a canine point of view. I assured her that after a few weeks and several thousand voice corrections, Luke would undoubtedly redeem himself as a good and gentle member of the family. Lisa, I'm afraid, would not be convinced that such a transformation could possibly take place. She decided instead to place Luke up for adoption—again.

With several thousand years of experience under our belts, why are we still having trouble with the concept that puppies teethe? Why are millions of puppy "parents" frustrated by this very natural aspect of puppy raising, and why are so many human children fleeing for their lives as they run helter-skelter through their own homes screaming, "Mommy, the puppy is trying to kill me!"? Because we're human and they are dogs, that's why.

If I had one wish for all puppies about to embark on the "human experience," it would be for each one to come with a short manual stating: "I am not aggressive, or malicious, manipulative, or mischievous. I am simply a member of a species that learns to hunt, earn the respect of its peers, and ultimately survive through the art of play. I possess teeth (that often double as hands) but, with them, bear you no ill will. I have an insatiable need to prove my keen abilities as a hunter, therefore showing you just how valuable a family member I can be. If you have a problem with this (my only known method of communication), simply teach me another way. I am a quick study. If I don't get it the first time, simply repeat the lesson until I behave as you wish."

Bringing up a puppy does have its parallels with bringing up human children. The development process of a dog, however, is almost ten times faster than that of a human child. Bearing this in mind makes it easier to remember that the puppy has far less time to make mistakes and that each stage of development is over almost as quickly as it begins. Because teething without guidance fosters "mouthy" behavior in the adult dog, I strongly recommend guidance from the outset.

Teething is the single most frustrating behavior we have to endure while living with a puppy. It can not only drive you stark, raving mad but it can also really hurt. It is not, however, malicious behavior and in no way should be interpreted as aggressive. Torn clothes and chewed furniture, not to mention bloodied hands, are side effects of the puppy's developmental process, not casualties of war. Milk teeth are a pup's god-given tools and with them he learns to hunt, tear food, and assert his strength as a healthy member of the pack. Remember Darwin and his thoughts about "survival of the fittest"? Well, teething is part of survival in its most primal and pure form.

Puppies will often bloody each other in play and walk away no worse for wear. They're happy to play the same game with you. Just watch two pups play and you'll be amazed by what you can learn. When a puppy of superior strength plays with another puppy of lesser strength and exerts too much of his power, the weaker pup won't hang around for long. This teaches the stronger pup not to use so much force the next time around because, if he does, he will lose his playmate.

With this in mind, if your puppy is using his mouth on you in an unacceptable manner, with unacceptable force, simply remove yourself (promptly) from the game and he will eventually learn that whenever his teeth come into the equation, the game is over. Play is a puppy's most valuable developmental pastime, and if "mouthing" inadvertently signals the end of a good game, the puppy will eventually learn not to use his mouth if he wants the game to continue. But, on the other hand, if you sit there and take it, your tolerance not only promotes the behavior, it also lets the pup know that if he uses his mouth, the game continues.

Some puppies have less of a teething drive while others have an insatiable need to mouth anything and everything in their line of sight. It might surprise you to learn that a puppy who is an insatiable teether often becomes the most gentle adult because he has been constantly reminded not to use his/her mouth. This (like all behavioral modification) requires guidance from you. The more a puppy uses his mouth inappropriately, the more he is (or should be) corrected for doing so and, as a result, he learns not to use his mouth inappropriately later in life.

If you have a monster teether, don't despair, just keep reminding your youngster that the behavior is not acceptable (with a voice correction—i.e., *no biting*) and remove your body part or valuable and replace it with an acceptable chew toy, praising the dog when he chooses (even by accident) to chew something that belongs to him and not you. Never strike a puppy on the face for using its mouth. Dogs use their mouths to communicate comfort as well as discomfort, and striking a young dog will only cultivate fearful or even aggressive behavior. Many dogs interpret a hand coming at them as the starting bell for a good boxing match, and what starts out as a correction from you escalates into all-out chaos. Your patience and control during this time are mandatory. When teething is approached as a natural (though ultimately unacceptable) developmental process, eventually the snapping crocodile does become a gentle dog and teething becomes a thing of the past.

Be careful not to unintentionally foster mouthing by allowing it simply because the object of your puppy's desire is old (and I don't mean your grandmother) or has little personal value (like an old shoe). Dogs don't discriminate between old furniture and new furniture or expensive shoes and worn-out shoes. Supply ample canine-specific chew toys and allow your puppy access to them whenever possible, and whatever you do, DO NOT play tug-of-war. It teaches a dog the strength of his own jaws and *Jaws* is what you will get if you make pulling a contest in which the winner has the strongest teeth. There are many bonding rituals, and chewing on your possessions or body parts does not have to be one of them.

As for teething in general, don't allow a little thing like a set of razor-sharp teeth come between you and the love you expected to feel for your dog. Many people misinterpret teething as a deliberate act of malice and, unfortunately, give puppies away because they can't ever imagine that the teething will subside. The up side is that I have yet to meet a person with a well-behaved adult dog who even remembers the traumas of teething, so hang in. The best is yet to come and you might even find yourself lovingly reminiscing about this short-lived toddler stage.

Most of us can honestly say that we wholeheartedly adore our dogs and have since the moment they came into our lives. But for some, love is a process that comes with time—if at all. Love is often an emotion that needs to be cultivated between two very distinct personalities. Sometimes the cultivation process becomes an emotional struggle that switches between "I cannot live without a dog" and "What on earth was I thinking when I decided to get a dog?" The result is too often a spoiled human/dog relationship—unless, of course, we change our expectations.

"The Best-Laid Plans . . ."

Allison was battling a debilitating disease and several of her friends and doctors suggested she get a dog as a therapeutic measure. She had always wanted a dog and agreed that the distraction of caring for another life as well as the companionship that she craved were perfect reasons for her to own a dog.

Sport, a two-year-old Border collie, had been living at a local veterinarian's office for about two months and was in need of companionship as well. There was little information about Sport's history other than that he had spent his two years of life with a family who had decided, after their second child was born, that a dog was not fitting into their family plan. When Allison heard about him, she felt this was the perfect opportunity and adopted Sport after just one short meeting.

The trouble began almost immediately. Allison's expectations of the ways in which living with a dog would ultimately change her life clashed with Sport's need to behave like the dog he was. Because Sport had already been abandoned by his first family, or pack, he was extremely wary of being abandoned again. He was also very sensitive about being socially accepted by a new pack. Following Allison from room to room helped to ease this fear. Because Sport had a strong herding instinct, nipping at Allison's heels and, ultimately, her hands and arms became another source of comfort—at least for the dog.

Even though the woman felt an instant love for and sense of devotion to her new partner, she found herself constantly battling behavior that she found "wicked" and "hurtful." Allison's arms were eventually so bruised that a friend commented about her "treatment" leaving her so marked and she replied that her bruises were not a result of any medical treatment at all but, in fact, of Sport's treatment of her. She was, sadly, not at all sure their relationship could or would endure his malevolent behavior. She had reached a point where she could admit out loud that she didn't even like this dog that she had fully intended to love. What Allison didn't know was that Sport was not being beastly at all, he was just fulfilling a need to keep Allison in plain sight at all times. Were Allison's doctors and friends wrong in their advice or was Allison just clueless about how to live with a dog?

When living with and having a relationship with another species, an understanding of how that species develops and lives its life lends volumes of information that can lead to the ultimate success of that relationship. If and when the group is broken up (i.e., we leave the house to go to work—for some dogs, your going out for the mail is all it takes—or go away for the weekend), the dog interprets your absence as a weakness in the group's overall stability. Once you arrive home, the dog is so overjoyed about the pack being whole again that joy often eclipses good sense and even training. It's as if the dog is saying, "Oh my god, you did come back!"

In Allison and Sport's case, neither was aware of the other's needs. Allison needed a dog to wait patiently at home all day while she went to work, especially as she was clearly exhausted when she finally got home. Sport, on the other hand, needed a pack. Some people say "secondhand" dogs make the most loyal pets. I, too, believe this to be true, but, because of their unbending need to stay "in touch" with other pack members, they are more susceptible to behavioral disorders like separation anxiety. And, because he was a herding dog, Sport had an even stronger need to "keep it together" whenever Allison was in the house. He in no way meant to harm her; he was simply herding her.

Thankfully, the solution to Allison and Sport's problem was not to end their relationship but, rather, to clarify it. Theirs was yet another case of great expectations gone awry. Allison had been relying on this relationship as a kind of medicine to heal her. What she had not counted on was that the medicine (her dog) needed healing as well. After speaking with several professional trainers and a canine behaviorist, Allison began to realize the importance of her role, not just as a pack member but as a pack leader.

Letting her dog know that she was in charge (through basic obedience exercises) relieved Sport of the impossible job of taking care of her. Keeping him busy (via obedience commands) gave Sport a job that diverted his energy from herding to listening. He began to follow Allison from room to room because she commanded him to—not because he was afraid she was going to leave him. Whenever Allison needed rest, she commanded Sport to rest ("settle down") as well. Because the dog was obeying the leader of his pack, this rest, unlike a voluntary rest, became part of this dog's job as a pack member and required effort. This effort tired him and helped to burn off his excess energy.

In essence, whenever Allison and Sport were together, Allison was telling Sport what to do. Instead of keeping her close, she was keeping him close, and instead of the dog worrying that Allison wouldn't return whenever she was away from home, the dog would simply rest. Whenever Allison returned home, the dog would have to work, kind of like Allison working days and Sport working nights. Allison was amazed by the change in Sport's behavior. Instead of mauling her with affection and an overzealous herding technique when Allison arrived home each evening, Sport was ready to work. He was happy to follow her commands and even happier to be a valuable, working member of his pack. As for Allison, she was just plain happy. Her doctors even noticed the change. After all was said and done, this dog was, in fact, good medicine.

Whether you live with a secondhand dog who's past is a puzzle or a weekend dog who spends most of its time lying in wait, give your dog a real job. Give your dog legitimate work when you are around and he will rest (and not worry) when you are gone. For people too busy during the day to deal with their dogs behavioral issues at night, and for dogs too bored during the day to behave around their people in the evening, this seems a fair and just compromise. It saved Allison's relationship with her dog just as it might save yours.

Have you ever heard the expression "Never judge someone until you have walked in his shoes"? Many years ago, a friend used it with me when I criticized another woman's parenting technique. The woman, whom I did not know, had been yelling at her child in public and I was nothing short of appalled! "How could this mother show such an inappropriate lapse in self-control?" I snapped. When my friend admonished me about judging, I smugly replied that I would never show such lack of control, regardless of the circumstances. Ten years and two children later, I wish I could track down that woman and apologize for my self-righteous cluelessness.

All dog owners could learn a lesson from this story. Don't be too quick to criticize the man who is being pulled down the street by his dog until you have had the hair-raising experience of being dragged by your own dog. We would all be a little better off, not to mention more tolerant, if we could take a moment to put ourselves in someone else's place. The chances are fair that we might just end up there ourselves someday. On the other hand, though, instead of making excuses for everyone's behavior, the fact is that we should all be a lot more careful about how we raise our animals.

Beast of Burden

Question: How do you love an obnoxious dog? *Answer:* The same way you love a well-behaved dog but with a lot of excuses.

A few months ago, I was training in Central Park in New York City and a young man came careening down one of the paved tributaries, dragged along by his dog. The dog, a chocolate Labrador retriever, was so out of control that he was both a danger to his owner and to anyone else who might have gotten in his way. I stood motionless, observing (something I try to do these days rather than judge), and this dog decided I was a wonderful target and headed straight for me. He jumped, hitting me square in the shoulders, and knocked me to the ground. The young man was so overwhelmed by the dog's strength that he couldn't even offer to help me up. He did however, offer an excuse for the dog's behavior. "I'm sorry," he told me, "he's very young." "Judging" (hey, nobody's perfect) from the animal's size, "young" was the last adjective I would have chosen to describe this dog, and once back on my feet, I just had to ask. "Exactly how 'young' is he?" "He's two," the young man replied. "Two? As in two years? That's not young, that's obnoxious!" This was what I wanted to say, but instead I told the owner: "Great-looking dog!"

Sound familiar? Well, it should, because we've all been there. You know, the neighbor's dog who jumps up on the side of your car door as you slow down to say hello to his owner. You're consumed with the knowledge that this dog is scratching the hell out of your car's paint job while the owner just stands there talking about the weather! Your first inclination is to floor it and leave the dog (and the owner) in the dust or, at the very least, swat the dog off your door like a fly, but instead you continue on the course of polite social intercourse.

At what point does a parent of a child or an owner of a dog begin to take responsibility for that child or that dog's actions? To this I say—as nonjudgmentally as possible—"From day one!"

Without guidance and instruction, young animals will not learn right from wrong and acceptable from unacceptable. As caretakers and providers, it becomes our responsibility to raise good citizens. Because there are all kinds of personalities and genetic traits that factor into the equation of child rearing, guidance and instruction become the only concrete method of molding good behavior. For those who believe that "youth" is an excuse for poor behavior and that our youngsters will simply "grow out of it," failure is pretty much guaranteed. For those, however, who believe that guidance transcends even the most obnoxious behavior, success is probably closer than you dare to think.

Many of my clients begin the task of raising a dog hoping to end up with something more like a soldier than a family pet. This is just fine, although a bit of a challenge if your life is not primarily devoted to training a dog. Many more of my clients, however, begin their dog training with the intention of treating their animal like nothing less than a blood relative of the royal family. For these folks, whatever behavior their pet demonstrates, however extreme, will be unconditionally accepted (see chapter 6, "The Brat Pack"). While the choice is a personal one, it seems clear that falling somewhere in the middle of these alternatives is the best plan. Maybe we should all set our sights on teaching all dogs to be, at the very least, good citizens. If we teach good manners and obedience at the same time, it would be easier for the dog to live with himself and easier for everyone else to live with the dog.

These days, when lawsuits are tossed around as freely as balls for our dogs to fetch, one must be very careful about one's own dog's overall behavior. Conversely, we also live in an age when we have begun to anthropomorphize the status of our dogs, making it even more difficult to decipher what we ultimately expect of their behavior. This has become an issue for serious debate.

Let's face it. We all want perfect children and perfect dogs—the kind that never question our decisions, no matter how inconvenient the follow-through may be. But this kind of relationship does not come cheap. It takes work. The kind of work that requires an understanding of the creature you are parenting. To begin with, raising dogs and children has never been an exact science, and raising the latchkey dog has become a phenomenon in and of itself.

With expectations of the human-canine relationship at an all-time high, the window for teaching well-mannered behavior has all but closed. Far too many of us are making far too many excuses ("because we love them . . .") for our dogs when we should instead be taking responsibility. But, with our emotions running dangerously close to the fever point, being the caretaker of the modern dog has begun to put many of us in uncomfortable, not to mention compromising, positions.

Most of a dog's behavior is species specific. Some behavior is due to genetics and/or breed, but quite a large portion is the product of environment. That being the case, let's talk about environment. Regardless of the breed(s) you ultimately choose to spend your life with, all dogs come with a strong, built-in set of instinctual rules. Everything else is taught.

Puppies need to be taught and guided through the challenges of growing up in a predominantly human environment. Adult and second-hand dogs need to be retaught, redirected, and reminded about the rules governing their new households. Without guidance and redirection, dogs will, in fact, just be dogs. So, the bottom line is, if you expect your dog to be well mannered and well behaved, expect yourself to be doing the teaching.

The sooner the teaching starts, the sooner the good citizen emerges. Youth is an absolutely reasonable excuse for some unattractive behavior but youth (as we all know) is fleeting and relying on "He's just a puppy" won't cut it for long. The most important thing to remember is that, regardless of your dog's age, if his behavior is unattractive by your standards, the chances are that it's unacceptable—or even insufferable—by someone else's. And, once the dog is an adult, his bad habits will elicit hostility and resentment from those around him. This is a heavy burden to place on any dog.

What begins as your responsibility ultimately falls on the shoulders of the dog himself. The result can be devastating to the outcome of a dog's life. This is the greatest reason for the astoundingly high population of dogs in shelters. You don't want them and neither does anybody else.

So, now that we have discussed just a few of the emotional pitfalls of great expectations, let's discuss how to avoid them.

• Try not to place too much weight on relationships that are not yet fully formed. Setting impossible standards only guarantees disaster. Make your commitment to your dog a lifelong one. If you are judging the length of the relationship on the ease of its flow, the chances are that the relationship will not last.

• Don't forget to allow room for error. No "parent" is perfect and parenting is a process, not an instantaneous pass or fail.

• If you change an existing house rule (i.e., no more lying on the living room couch), be consistent with the rule change and expect the dog to test what he thinks is your own temporary confusion about the rules ("What do you mean 'off'? this is my couch!"). Stick to your guns and the dog will soon accept the change rather painlessly.

• Remember not to use youth as an excuse; use it as an opportunity. Begin teaching the "house rules" as early as the day the dog comes to live with you. If you don't want the sixty-pound dog jumping on your shoulders, don't let the twelve-pound puppy jump on your knees. If you don't want to share your meals with the dog when dinner guests are visiting, don't share your meals with the dog when the two of you are alone.

• Remind yourself (daily) that mistakes are a necessary part of learning (for you and the dog)—how else are you both supposed to learn how not to do something? For example: If your puppy (who you thought was housebroken) has just soiled the kitchen floor, rejoice. Yes, I did say rejoice. As long as you have witnessed the "flood gates" opening, it is a perfect opportunity to let the puppy know that, under no circumstances—even if he has to—is he to use the house as a toilet. The next time he has to "go," he might just wait until you take him outside.

• Set realistic goals and remember, all good things do not come to those who wait, they come to those who go out and get them. Don't wait for the dog to stop chewing the living room carpet, tell him it's not acceptable (with a voice correction), and then let him know what he can chew. This way, the next time he feels the "call of the wild," he will pick something of his own to destroy . . . you hope.

If your relationship with your dog has failed to meet your expectations, change your expectations, not your dog. We are, after all, supposed to be in charge here.

Chapter 9

Midlife Crisis

When Your Emotions Run Away with the Dog's Behavior

People get dogs for all kinds of reasons, reasons they are often not even aware of, and ultimately the relationships they have with their dogs are affected by these reasons.

Perhaps you've taken stock of your life and your "ten-year plan" is not exactly on schedule. Maybe you're remembering the good times you had with the dog you had as a kid. Or, maybe your own children have been begging you to get a dog. Your parents did it—so why not you, right? Whatever the reason, you decide it's time, so you get the dog.

Six months later, you're tearing your hair out. You can't get the dog to do what you say. You can't get the dog to stop chewing your valuables. You can't get the dog to stop jumping on your friends. Basically, you just can't get any peace when you're with the dog. And if that's not bad enough, when you're apart, your mind is so consumed with guilt for leaving him alone that you just can't get any peace when you're not with the dog. Before long, your dream of sharing your life with a dog has become a midlife crisis.

Believe it or not, little about the responsibility of owning a dog has really changed. It's the way in which we are relating to our dogs that has changed. The basic principles of dog rearing still hold as true today as they did several hundred years ago and, as hard as it may be to believe, your mother (or father, as the case may be) had to conquer the same "doggy" dilemmas that you now face. Being a child (as you were then) in a household that included a dog is very different indeed than being the parent in that same household. Now, however, you are the parent and the responsibility is more enormous than you imagined.

Rethinking your life's plan and contemplating where you went wrong or reevaluating your status as a dog owner are all a waste of time. Instead, try taking things one step at a time. To begin with, all living creatures go through developmental stages. For dogs, infancy to adulthood all take place in the amazingly short span of eighteen months. So, if you're starting with a puppy, plan ahead for—at the very least—an action-packed year and a half. (That is not to say that some adult dogs don't need constant guidance as well.)

Going into this commitment with your eyes wide open makes living with any dog easier and coping with each developmental stage a short-term challenge instead of a long-term disaster (see chapter 8, "Great Expectations"). No dog, even the one that lived with you as a kid, was problem-free. Someone (and it was probably your mother) worked very hard to incorporate that dog into the family. There's little doubt about it, behind every well-behaved dog is a person who taught him to be that way.

Achy, Breaky Heart

A young woman recently called me for some advice about her thirteen-week-old dalmatian puppy. She had had the dog for only one week but was already about to throw in the towel. "The puppy," she said, "didn't like her." Every time she tried to pet him, he bit her. And, she said, if he wasn't biting her, he was pawing at her. She interpreted the "pawing" as pushing her away and was devastated that the dog did not want to be with her. She went on to explain that she had had dogs most of her life when she lived at home with her family but that their behavior was nothing like this.

Her decision to get her own dog was based partially on the fact that she was recovering from an eating disorder and thought that having a dog to care for and love might distract her from her own problems. She had a clear picture in her head of how this relationship would unfold and was not at all prepared for the dog's "feelings" not to match her own. Having lived with dogs before, she didn't feel it was necessary to "read up" on dog training or dog behavior. Instead, she was taking whatever advice she could get (and it was plenty) from whoever felt the need to offer it.

One person said rawhide was an absolute "no-no" because "all dogs who chew rawhide choke and die." Another suggested leaving the dog for several hours at a time because "dogs need to get adjusted to a new home—alone and without the distraction of people." And another even suggested that holding a young puppy in your arms would only send "mixed messages" about going to the bathroom on the street when it came time to housebreak the dog. I thought I had heard just about everything, but even the thought that there were people walking the streets giving out this kind of free advice chilled me to my spine. Anyway, the bottom line was that this grown woman needed more therapy now than before she got the dog. And, even worse, this dog was doomed to a life of utter confusion.

How, and I ask myself this question more often than I care to admit, can a person get a dog without the slightest understanding of the "make" and "model" they are about to commit an average of ten years of their life to? The fact is, the number of people sharing their lives with dogs and having little knowledge of how to live with a dog is staggeringly high. But even more frightening are the reasons for people choosing to get a dog in the first place. "Coming of age" does not necessarily come with a free pass to take on the responsibility of parenting, and parenting a dog is definitely a serious responsibility. So before you run off half-cocked and pick a dog, why not arm yourself with a few facts first?

• All dogs need to be taught how they are expected to behave. None (and I mean none) of this behavior comes automatically—the stuff that comes automatically to a dog (i.e., chewing, barking, digging) is usually the stuff that drives you crazy.

• Whenever a dog begins a relationship with a human, kinks need to be ironed out before the relationship will run smoothly and this can and often does take many weeks if not months.

• Each dog is an individual and has its own distinct personality, making some dogs (like some people) more difficult to live with than others.

• Although training methods go in and out of fashion as often as the height of hem lines, the rules of fundamental dog parenting do not. Ask your mother—I'd be willing to bet that the reality of how much work it added to her daily routine is still quite fresh in her mind.

Even those who have a pretty good idea of what it takes to parent a dog are often completely blindsided by the emotional interference that jams up the mechanism of even the simplest training process. When a person who measures his or her own life in terms of accomplishments (and counts owning a dog as one of them) decides to finally get a dog, the play between good sense and sensibility should be dealt with beforehand.

Here are a few examples of the struggle between good sense and excess emotion.

• "Will the dog understand that I still love her even if I tell her she can't chew the legs off my dining room chairs?"

- "Why must I make my dog 'sit' for his food if it doesn't really matter to me if he sits for his food or not?"

- "Okay, so my dog is a bit aggressive toward strangers and other dogs but, when it's just the two of us, he's so sweet."

- "Why do I have to continually remind my dog that I am the pack leader? I didn't get this dog to push her around—I just want to love her."

- "So he likes to chew the rug—I'll get another rug."

Sound familiar? Our responses to our dogs are becoming more visceral and less intellectual. This, in my opinion, greatly contributes to many of our modern dog's behavioral problems. Perhaps it is because so many of us now spend the greater portion of our days in the workplace, being intellectually challenged, that we feel the need to let our hair down once we get home. But, because the dog does not have a clue that you are indulging him for the preservation of your own sanity, a balance should be found. But, as we dive headfirst into the deep, emotional pool of dog love, the balance, I fear, is becoming harder and harder to find.

Peter and the Wolf

Peter, a forty-seven-year-old CEO of his own software company, was having trouble with his eighteen-month-old Akita, Aki. Peter had hired me to help him train Aki when she was just a puppy. He had read a few training books prior to getting the dog and wanted to be a responsible dog owner. Peter was divorced and did not have any children. He often thought about settling down and having a family but his career left him little time to socialize. He had never had a dog before but, when he was a child, a friend of his had a great dog of whom he had always been envious. Eventually, Peter decided, if he couldn't have the family and the kids, he could at least have the dog . . . and then there was Aki.

When I first met Peter, I was delighted to learn that he had really done his "homework." There was little about the fundamentals of dog training that he was not familiar with, at least in theory. We met an average of once a week for a few weeks, taking care of the basics and, after that, only sporadically to deal with normal issues that present themselves with each new stage of canine development. Peter was enthusiastic about spending time with and training his puppy, and Aki had developed into a generally well-behaved dog—that is, except for a couple of "tiny" problems.

For all of Peter's efforts to educate himself about dogs, he was totally unprepared for the emotional turmoil that this dog had brought into his life. He had become so attached to Aki, crediting her for giving his life new meaning (for the first time in years he had stopped obsessing about a family because this dog was now his family), that he was fast becoming incapable of separating fact from feeling. Even the most elementary training techniques were being clouded by emotion. He no longer felt comfortable telling this dog what to do. The dog, of course, sensed the man's discomfort and began to behaviorally unravel.

If Aki began to chew the carpet or the leg of a chair, Peter simply weighed the value of the objects against the value of his relationship with his dog and quickly decided the objects were not worth the upset caused by an obedience lesson. If Aki lunged at another dog on the street, Peter made excuses to himself and the other dog owners in order to sidestep any awkward situations. And, to make matters worse, if anyone commented on the dog's behavior, Peter took the criticism as one might take criticism of his own child. He understood intellectually why Aki needed to be taught how to behave like a good citizen (and what it took to help her become one) but, in his heart, he simply could not accept that he had to constantly correct her. "She's a dog," he'd tell himself. "Why can't I just let her be a dog?" His words were more a statement than a question.

Explaining to someone who is overly emotionally invested in a dog that good sense should overrule emotion is like explaining to a new mother that she should let her baby cry because someone else said it's good for the baby. The point is, no matter who the advice comes from, such advice feels counterintuitive and therefore often seems too difficult to follow through on. In situations like this, and there are far more than you can imagine, trying to reason is often pointless.

Damn the Message, Shoot the Messenger

Not long ago, I worked with a woman named Jackie and her (in my opinion) very aggressive young chow chow, Brutus. Jackie had purchased Brutus from an out-of-state breeder, sight unseen. Although she was a bit surprised by his intolerant nature toward strangers, having never owned a dog, she chalked up her fears to her own canine naiveté and proceeded to quickly fall head over heels in love with her new little "man."

When we first met, Brutus was fourteen weeks old and already showing signs of fear aggression. It was unclear whether he had been improperly bred, abused, or was just plain scared. I warned Jackie that I was concerned that a young dog possessing such a guarded nature needed to be trained immediately and trained well. Without a specific set of rules for this dog to rely on, his aggression would only get worse.

We talked about some of the training and behavioral modification possibilities that I thought might help Brutus to "relax" a bit. Jackie and Brutus lived alone, so first I explained that this dog must always know that he was not in charge of this pack of two. Then Jackie let me know, in no uncertain terms, that she was uncomfortable with any technique that might require, as she put it, "domesticating her dog." I knew then that Jackie and I were not the perfect match as teacher and student.

I am not and have never been an advocate of using brute force to train any dog. But because dogs are creatures that communicate through body language, "brute force" to one dog may be interpreted as child's play to another. For dogs who require stronger boundaries (i.e., dogs with aggressive tendencies), speaking their own physical language (i.e., you crossing the threshold of a doorway first, not the dog; making the dog work for his food with a "sit-stay" first; never allowing these dogs to leave the ground; etc.) actually calms them. These dogs absolutely and without question need clearer boundaries to keep them sane.

Anyway, because Jackie did not have a lot of confidence in my advice, I urged her to get a second opinion and hoped that I was wrong about her dog.

Jackie did get a second and, in fact, a third opinion. Her veterinarian told her that Brutus was just a "wild puppy" who needed a "firm hand." Another vet, I dare say, leaned a bit more my way in his diagnosis of Brutus's personality, but did not, in any case, brand the dog as potentially dangerous . . . at least for now. Jackie felt comfortable that this information (which she obviously wanted to hear) was correct, and she went home with Brutus happy to disregard my diagnosis and training advice.

We met only once more (I think Jackie wanted to show me that I had been wrong about her dog), when Brutus was almost six months old. By now he had grown to lean, mean, fighting-machine size and when I stepped off the elevator, Jackie and Brutus were there to greet me. Brutus was busy lunging at a man's arm, and once the man disappeared into the elevator, Brutus began lunging at me. As she did nothing to let the dog know that the lunging was not a desirable behavior, I firmly instructed Jackie to get the dog under control. This, I fear, did not set the proper stage for our next and last session together.

During our session, Jackie did tell me about an incident that had occurred some days before in the elevator of her apartment building. It had involved a small child in a stroller and, you guessed it, Brutus. Jackie described the incident as isolated. (I think Jackie was once again attempting to convince me, or perhaps herself, that Brutus's behavior was not problematic.) Anyway, Brutus, it seemed, had lunged at the baby—"out of curiosity," Jackie assured me. The stroller was about four inches farther away than the end of the dog's leash and, for no apparent reason, Brutus wanted to "have a look." Fortunately, Jackie was able to pull the dog away. Nothing happened to the child but, if it had not been for the short length of the dog's leash, I still contend something would have. Although Jackie listened to my warnings that her dog's dangerously bold demeanor would not soften with age but would instead grow worse, she had already taken irreparable, personal offense to my criticism of her dog and, as she put it, had been *frightened by my candor.* There was little hope for the survival of our partnership so we went our separate ways.

In all fairness, I must say that I actually understand how Jackie could feel this way. I had, after all, told her that the canine love of her life might be damaged goods. Nobody wants to hear that from anybody, no matter how much that person claims to know. Denouncing me personally and professionally was the only way for this woman to live with this dog and not have to, as she put it, "domesticate" him. But the fact still remains, denying that the problem exists is the last thing that's going to help the problematic dog.

Whether the crisis is yours or your dogs', finding a realistic resolution to the quandary of dog rearing has become a problem in and of itself. Love is not easily compartmentalized but dog behavior must be. When the two (love and dog behavior) are combined, compromise is often the only winner. Compromise though, however comforting it may be to you, is only confusing for the dog.

Adding a dog to your life should be (and often is) a wonderful, enriching experience for both you and the dog. Relying on a dog to change the status of your life or fulfill a void in your life is a pretty tall order—one most dogs are not cut out to fill. The solution to avoiding the pitfalls of a midlife crisis often lies in a simple system of checks and balances.

If your dog's behavior is even questionable, first check your own behavior toward the dog. Are you allowing or perhaps even promoting the behavior in question? If you are, first try to reset realistic expectations of the relationship, then retrain the dog. Balance is found when you can honestly say you are proud of and comfortable with the dog's overall behavior. If you find yourself walking the dog over to the other side of the street rather than allowing a natural social encounter (whenever you are outside your own home) because you feel you might not be able to control your dog, its time to recheck the dynamic that exists between you and the dog when you are at home. If your dog is not required to follow instructions at home, he is not going to look to you for direction when faced with the distractions of the outside world.

Avoiding emotional pitfalls with your dog by keeping your own behavior in check will help you to avoid getting caught smack in the middle of a midlife canine crisis. You will only get out of your dog's behavior what you put into it. If halfway is all that you can muster in the directives department, then halfway is all you're going to get out of your dog's follow-through.

If Peter had been willing to let his dog, Aki, know that certain of his possessions were "off-limits" to her in the first place, then Aki would have had a clearer picture of what she could and could not destroy. It's that simple. And, if Jackie had been willing to show a little tough love by not allowing Brutus to think he was ruling their roost, then Brutus would undoubtedly have felt the need to be a little less tough. Those who vacillate between practicality and emotion (as when it applies to living with a dog) will eventually have to spell out the rules for that dog anyway. If they don't, the relationship becomes chaotic and ultimately spins totally out of control, leaving the dog with a disgusted partner and, in many cases, no partner at all.

Peter and Jackie are just two of the millions of modern dog owners who have voluntarily opted for an abridged version of the obedient dog. Much like the owners of brat dogs (chapter 6), they would rather let their dogs "be a little naughty" than struggle with their own conscience about such mundane matters as dog training. It is, in a manner of speaking, their own way of coping with a midlife crisis.

This alone is why so many people are beginning to expect less of their own, not to mention everybody else's, dog's behavior. Perhaps it's just a momentary trend or maybe it's the new precedent—I'm not sure, but I'm hoping it's the former. Either way, sometimes the head (even when it is attached to the shoulders of a dog trainer) is just no match for the heart.

Rites of Passage

For those of us whose hearts belong (even in part) to our own dogs, there's yet another matter that deserves its own bit of attention. With more and more of us investing our time, money, and lives in our relationships with our dogs, it's a good idea to think about what might happen to those dogs given the fact that something might happen to us first. Not the most pleasant topic I agree, but somebody's got to bring it up.

A close friend (not a dog lover at all) was thinking about getting her aging mother a companion dog. She thought long and hard about it, researched a breed that she, and her mother, decided would be compatible with her mother's lifestyle, and enlisted a promise of help from me if behavioral issues should arise.

During one of our many preparatory conversations about the prospects of the success of this venture, I advised my friend to consider the dog's age when choosing the actual dog. She questioned me as to why the age of the dog would make any difference and I explained. Given the fact that a young dog was more than likely going to outlive her mother, the probability was great that that dog might then actually belong to her. Astonished that she had overlooked the possibility that she might end up being an honest-to-goodness dog owner herself, she began to rethink the whole idea. It was, after all, her mother who wanted the dog, not she. Fortunately, the whole thing was resolved when my friend, after discussing it with her mother, decided to adopt an "older" dog and, just in case, found a family friend (who could provide an appropriate home) who agreed to take the dog should the need arise.

This is just one more predicament being faced by modern dog owners that is more common than one cares to admit. After all, nobody wants to face the facts about their own mortality. In spite of this, more and more of us are taking dogs into our lives without a master plan for the future. Even a new relationship (chapter 2, "Role over Rover") can change the course of destiny between you and your dog—a job transfer, an unexpected baby in the house, or maybe an allergic child of a new spouse. The reasons are too numerous to cite but, the bottom line is: It could happen, and it does happen. Many older people, too, are losing long time canine companions and replacing them with puppies or young dogs that will probably outlive their caretakers. Creating a parachute for these dogs, in the event of your untimely demise, is just another aspect of responsible dog parenting.

Without citing the legalese of how your last will and testament should read, simply stated—don't forget the dog. Whether you ask a friend to agree to take on the responsibility or appoint an honest-to-goodness legal guardian, it's the only way to go (no pun intended).

Chapter 10

Size Really Does Matter

Choosing a Dog

Many people decide to get a dog about five minutes before they actually do so. You pass by the window of the pet shop and there she is! The cutest little face you ever saw. You tell yourself you just want a closer look and, instantly, you're hooked. Congratulations . . . you just got a puppy! Anyone who tells you this has never happened to them is obviously not a card-carrying dog lover. Add to this those of us who just can't stay away from the dog shows or the shelters or those heartwrenching "needs a loving home" want ads in the newspaper. An acquaintance went out shopping

*for a new refrigerator and came home with a dog.
Eleven years later, the dog is still running and she
can't recall why she wanted a new refrigerator anyway. The fact is, anyone who has ever believed (even
for a moment) that Lassie should have been their dog
is eventually going to get a dog.*

    *Choosing the right dog, however, can sometimes
be a tricky business. . . .*

About two years ago a client recommended that a woman call me to ask
if I knew of a reputable toy poodle breeder. She was very specific about
what she was looking for and, although I did not know of a breeder, I told
her how to find one. Several months later, to my surprise, the same
woman called to ask if I knew of any golden retriever breeders in her
area. I, of course, inquired about her search for a poodle and she replied
that she had found a breeder and, in fact, had purchased a puppy some
months back. Assuming that she was looking for a second dog, I gave her
some information on golden breeders.

    Several months later, I heard from the same woman again. This
time she was calling to ask if I could help her (yet again) choose the right
breed of dog for her family. When I inquired about the poodle and the
golden she told me that she had purchased both dogs but had decided
after "trying them out" for a few months that neither one seemed to be
what she was looking for. I must confess that, for the first time in my
life, I was speechless! Finally, I managed to find the words to ask what
had happened to the other two dogs. The woman very matter-of-factly
told me that she had given both dogs away. She explained that "they just
weren't for her." I instantly conjured up the picture of a big department
store sale, only instead of clothing, the store was selling dogs. There
were shoppers everywhere grabbing any dog they could get their hands
on, sizing them up, then tossing them aside as if they weren't the right
size or the right color. . . . For obvious reasons, I will always feel partially responsible for the fate of those two dogs.

    Anyone who has ever followed through on the decision to get a dog
knows all too well the magnitude of responsibility that comes with car-

ing for another life. Since we do not always have the luxury of choosing the people we live with, why not take advantage of the luxury (and it is clearly a luxury) of being able to *choose* the dogs we live with?

With a wealth of information at our fingertips, finding out that terriers are small-rodent chasers (so they might not be right for the home with several small human feet running around the house all day), and that herding dogs love to keep track of the kids, and that bulldogs can be extremely territorial when eating can be as easy as signing on-line. Doing your homework when "shopping" for a dog can save you a lifetime of aggravation, and for the dog, it might even save its life.

So, let's just say you are in the market for a dog. What do you do? Where do you look? Where do you begin?

The first and most important thing to do is to think about why you want a dog in the first place. Perhaps you have just lost a loved one and need companionship. Perhaps it's because the children want a dog. Is it because you want a child? Maybe you are searching for a roommate or maybe a soul mate. Whatever the reason, being honest with yourself about that reason will ultimately help lead you to the right dog. If the relationship is to be successful, taking into consideration the lifestyle you might eventually lead, not just the one you are living now, should also factor into the equation.

Determining why you want a dog will help to realistically determine your expectations of the relationship. For example, if you eventually want children but choose to begin by parenting a dog, it would be prudent to choose a breed of dog whose temperament is generally good with children. This way, when the real children arrive, the dog is more likely to take it all in stride and less likely to become a problem. These considerations can be applied to any situation.

Now comes the fun part. What breed(s) of dog would best suit the type of relationship you want? There are more than 100 dog breeds recognized by the American Kennel Club (AKC) alone and many more throughout the world. Some breeds have been around for thousands of years and the information about their specific physical characteristics and personality traits is well documented and will prove to be invaluable when looking for a dog with whom to share your life.

Dogs, as a species, share many of the same behavioral language skills. When separated by specific breed, however, they can prove to be quite different from one another—sort of like two people who share the same country of origin but speak different dialects of the same language. With hundreds of different types of domesticated dogs available, choosing a dog is not as simple as just choosing a pretty face. The dog who thrives down on the farm is not necessarily best suited to city living.

Don't be fooled into choosing a dog solely for its size. In fact, a dog's size should only come into play when considering how *big* it might be. In other words, you should chose a boxer not only because you have the living space, but also because you plan on spending a good deal of time exercising the dog. But, choosing a breed of dog because you are attracted to how *small* it is (i.e., choosing a Jack Russell terrier because you live in tight quarters and can carry it around in your arms) can prove to be a very large mistake. A dog's appearance can sometimes be dangerously deceptive. Many small dogs possess the courage of lions and will not tolerate being toted around in a Sherpa bag. Never, if you know what's good for you, judge a small dog by its size.

Hush, Hush, Sweet Charlotte . . .

Charlotte was a Lhasa apso whose owner, Rachel, decided on her particular breed because of its compact size. Rachel wanted her dog to be small enough that going to the bathroom (on paper) in the house would not be offensive. She spent long hours away from home and did not want her dog to have to hold her bladder and bowels for extended periods of time. She also wanted a dog that she could cuddle up with on the couch and carry around.

It wasn't long before Rachel discovered that Charlotte's personality did not match Charlotte's appearance at all. The dog was not very social with strangers and had a rather quick temper. She was also very noisy. So noisy, in fact, that the woman decided to give Charlotte back to her breeder. Rachel said she had no idea that Lhasas were quick tempered and noisy. If she had known, she never would have chosen this kind of dog.

Rachel is clearly not the only dog owner who has made a mistake with the breed of dog they have chosen to live with and, I dare say, given it back. Doing your homework and researching different breeds and breed traits can save you and your dog a lifetime of trouble.

To begin with, dog breeds are easiest to research when broken down by group. The groups are sporting, hounds, working, terriers, toys, nonsporting, and herding dogs. All of these dogs have been somewhat altered in behavior and appearance over the last seven hundred years or so by both breeding and evolution. Some breeds remain closer to their natural state than others but, for reasons of necessity and fashion, the majority have been bred quite deliberately to look and act a certain way. Most, however, have been bred to do a specific job.

As Shelby Marlo (dog trainer and author of *Shelby Marlo's New Art of Dog Training*) states, "For the most part, dog breeds fall into one of two categories: those bred to work with people and those bred to work independently." If you choose a dog that is bred to work independently (terriers and hounds, for example), they are less likely to need or heed your instruction and more likely to do what comes naturally. These dogs are generally more headstrong about following their own instinct instead of you. If, however, you choose a dog that has been bred to follow instruction (the working and sporting breeds), training and controlling behavior comes more easily. These dogs are natural team players and get pleasure out of working with and pleasing you.

I live with two dogs, one, a golden retriever named Scout that I have had since he was seven weeks old, and the other, a mixed-breed stray named Wylie that I believe was about two years old when we found him and might have some Australian shepherd and possibly some husky in him. Scout, the golden, is enormously attentive and very careful to stay close to at least one human family member at all times. He is reliable and very predictable in that he will never leave our property lines for fear that he might lose one of his people. Never has he strayed more than a few feet with his body or his mind. Scout (a retriever) is a dog that has been bred to work alongside a person.

Wylie, on the other hand, is a horse of a different color. He is affectionate, gentle, very intelligent, and very eager to please. That is, until and unless something catches his eye. Then, forget it—he's gone. He can scale an eight-foot fence faster than most dogs can run on level ground. His need to follow his instinct is far stronger than his need to work alongside anyone. It's almost as if his body and his mind are in a constant struggle over whether to follow orders or succumb to the call of the wild. I dare say the call of the wild usually wins.

I often think that Scout wishes he were more like Wylie. Whenever Wylie has been off on one of his "jaunts," then returns home, Scout spends hours smelling him all over, as if to gather clues about where his pack member has been. Perhaps the smell wafts its way into the depths of Scout's dog soul, allowing him to live vicariously through his daring, more adventurous friend—even if it is just a dog fantasy.

Wylie and Scout are a perfect example of two dogs that are species-related but as different in breed character as night and day. These factors should not only come into play but should carry a lot of weight when choosing a dog for your family.

Dog "breed" books offer a wealth of information on individual breed characteristics as well as specific health issues and should be viewed as *Consumer Reports* when looking for a dog. They can prove to be a veritable road map that, when used properly, can literally help steer you to a pot of gold at the end of a rainbow.

One such book is *Harper's Illustrated Handbook of Dogs* by Robert W. Kirk and Roger Caras. It is accurate in its brief descriptions of many of the breeds and includes information on ancestry, grooming, general health, and training needs. This book offers a great starting place and, once you've narrowed down the field, breed-specific books can help even more. Some other noteworthy books to check out are: *Paws to Consider—Choosing the Right Dog for You and Your Family*, by Brian Kilcommons and Sarah Wilson; *Choosing a Dog—Your Guide to Picking the Perfect Breed*, by Nancy Baer and Steve Duno, and *Dog Adoption: A Guide to Choosing the Perfect "Pre-owned" Dog from Breeders, Dog Tracks, Purebred Rescue Organizations & Shelters*, by Joan Hustace Walker. Doing your homework before picking a dog is like buying a mental-health insurance policy for both you and the dog.

Doing a site search on-line is another option. The information is updated frequently and offers a rich cross section of facts from general canine behavior to specific health-related information. The Internet puts volumes of valuable information at your fingertips. Simply sign on to a search engine and surf away.

The next step is to shop. I recommend that people literally go out and look at the different models. I don't mean to liken your dog search to car shopping; it is, in fact, quite a different enterprise. For one thing, you can test-drive a car—you can't test-drive a dog. You would never buy a car without looking under the hood, yet millions of us, each year, purchase dogs without a second thought to what it takes to maintain their physical as well as mental health. And, once you drive a car off the lot, you can't bring it back. Unfortunately, far too many dogs are returned for reasons that could have been avoided with a bit of research beforehand. Maybe getting a dog *should* be more like car shopping.

Once you have narrowed down your choices to a specific breed or breeds, it is time to decide where to get the dog. The choices are as follows: pet shop, shelter, rescue, or breeder.

Pet Shop Puppies

We have all seen and read the many exposés on puppy mills and the unethical practices of some pet shops. The idea that anyone could knowingly participate in such cruelty is deplorable, and patronizing these establishments perpetuates their practices, but the fact remains, it is so hard to resist that doggy in the window. As a consumer, the choice is yours to make, but, buyer, please beware. At the very least, many pet shop puppies are forced to spend long hours in cages that double as bathrooms as well as living quarters. This often reverses the natural instinct that a dog has to keep its sleeping area clean and can make for a messy housebreaking problem.

Some are even taken from their mothers at too early a stage in their development and this, too, can cause problems (i.e., aggression, separation anxiety, and obsessive behaviors) later in the game. So, for those of us who do become enamored of such a dog, let it be said that we are probably buying something other than what the pet shop proprietor tells us he or she is selling. Having said that, I think it's only fair to add that these dogs do need homes and (although many have problems hidden under their furry little coats) I, for one, have lived with, known, and had the privilege of working with many wonderful, well-rounded, intelligent, and healthy pet shop puppies. The fact remains, however, that buying a pet shop puppy is little more than a crapshoot.

Gimme Shelter

Adopting from a local shelter is another option, one I highly recommend. People who adopt dogs from shelters are to be commended, as they are doing nothing short of a saintly deed. Each year, millions of dogs are senselessly euthanized because there are just too many dogs and not enough homes for them. There are many purebred as well as mixed-breed dogs behind the walls of these city and state facilities who are literally lying in wait to be either adopted or destroyed. I'm sure you've heard the expression, "One man's trash is another man's treasure." Such is the case with shelter and rescue dogs. These dogs are or have the potential to be amazing, they just need the right people to bring out the best in them. Even the dog who has spent several months in a cage and suffers from shelter fatigue (withdrawn or antisocial behavior), blossoms when placed in the right environment.

Little or nothing is ever known for certain about a shelter dog's past, but it's safe to assume it probably wasn't good. For this reason, many people who choose to adopt one of these dogs try to make up for the dog's checkered past the moment they get him home. Difficult as it may be to believe, indulgence is not the medicine these dogs need—guidance is. Indulging them only opens the floodgates for further behavioral issues. A dog who is used to little or inappropriate attention, and is then suddenly showered with love and attention without being taught how to earn these things, becomes confused about his rank and responsibility within the pack. This might very likely be the reason he landed in a shelter in the first place. Be realistic about building this dog's self esteem through basic obedience, giving him a vehicle to prove his worth.

Separation anxiety and obsessive behaviors abound in shelter dogs. They have already been abandoned at least once before and are terribly gun-shy about being abandoned again. Be careful not to spend every waking moment with them—this fosters dependency, a dependency to which they are understandably vulnerable. Instead, teach them from the onset—with the "down" and "stay" commands, leaving them for only a moment and returning—that your absence is short-lived and that you will, in fact, always return.

Whether they have been carelessly bred, abused, or simply misunderstood, these dogs come with baggage, and a kind heart and good intentions are not always enough to get them over their past nightmares. It takes patience and sometimes previous dog experience to heal many of these dogs. Be realistic and open-minded when choosing a shelter dog, and, above all, remember: Taking the time to fix what has been broken in this dog's character and spirit will automatically unleash the great dog within.

Rescue Me

Rescue is another option. If you are interested in adopting a dog rather than purchasing one, but are specific about the breed of dog you would like to live with, each breed has its own specialty/rescue club. A specialty club is an organization whose interests and affection focus on a specific breed of dog. Each region has its own chapters and they almost always have dogs of that breed available for adoption. To locate a specialty club in the area closest to your own home, first contact the AKC (5580 Center View Drive, Raleigh, NC 27606, 919-233-9767) or go to the library and get the most recent November issue of the *AKC Gazette*. Once a year, they publish a list of rescue coordinators for each national breed club. Contact them for a local rescue coordinator. The chances are, these dogs come with a checkered past similar to the shelter dog, but knowing the overall behavioral traits of a specific breed can prove invaluable when bringing a stranger into your home.

Breeder's Choice

Now let's talk about breeders. If you have narrowed down your field of choices to a specific breed or breeds, it's time to look for a breeder. The first thing to do is to contact the AKC for the name and telephone number of the secretary of the breed club in your area. That person should be able to steer you to a specific breeder(s) in your area, as well as let you know of any upcoming dog shows at which you might have the opportunity to meet prospective puppy parents.

Be sure to give the breeder you have chosen as much information as possible about your lifestyle and how you intend to raise this puppy. A good breeder should actually require this information. Let the breeder help choose your puppy. Many people want to make their own choice and, unfortunately, that specific dog's personality might not be well suited to your living arrangements. An experienced breeder should be skilled at pairing the right dog with the right person.

Once you have decided on a breeder, gather as much information about him or her as you would about the puppies. Be careful to explore the breeder's reputation and breeding practices. Ask for references and follow up by contacting people who own puppies that came from this breeder. Not all breeders are responsible and cautious about their breeding and a good breeder will only appreciate your diligence—if they don't, simply take your business elsewhere.

Be sure to meet the parents of your puppy. After all, the apple really doesn't fall far from the tree and, if one or both of the parents are nasty, the chances are, your youngster has more than a bit of that in him as well. Ask about everything from longevity in the line to show and obedience titles in the past generations. It will help you to determine your dog's trainability quotient.

When to Buy

Find out at what age the breeder prefers to let the puppies go home with new families. Seven weeks (or forty-nine days) is the optimum age for *all* puppies to "leave the nest" and begin socialization with their new family and the outside world. Some breeders like to keep their puppies longer. Whether it is to keep an eye on which pups develop into "show" prospects or simply because they like to hang on to the puppies for a few weeks longer, seven weeks (but not before) is the preferable age for you to bring the puppy home.

I have found that many puppies who stay with their breeders for more than twelve weeks (an extremely sensitive socialization age) have a difficult time adjusting to new surroundings and new situations throughout their lives.

You, as the consumer, are entitled to as much information as you require. Don't be intimidated about asking questions. You have the right and the responsibility to ask them. The chances are, if the breeder doesn't have the patience required to answer your questions, he surely does not have the patience required to breed and raise dogs. If that is the case, find another breeder.

Buyer Beware

Are all dogs suited to all people? It is believed (of the domesticated dog) that all dogs should live with people—but should personality and environment be factored in when choosing a dog? Dog trainer and author Vicki Hearne says "Dogs, like people, have tremendous talents and affinities for—and antipathies to—certain kinds of landscapes and terrain, both literal and cultural." In other words, just because you choose to live with a specific breed of dog does not necessarily mean that that breed of dog is well suited to living with you. Many people do consider where they live and what they are looking for in the personality of a dog, but do they give it enough consideration? Too many people make the mistake of shopping for a "look" without considering the deep-rooted needs of some dogs. This can often cost you the relationship of your dreams, and it can cost the dog its life.

One such breed that comes to mind is the wheaton terrier. This dog has become enormously popular over the last decade, not only because of its size (not too big, not too small), but also because it is a nonshedding breed. So what could be so bad? Well, lately, plenty. These dogs were bred to be "all purpose" farm dogs. That means they herd, they hunt, and they protect. The wheaton is a highly intelligent dog. They do not necessarily fare well in small apartments, sitting around all day, waiting. In addition, it is believed that the wheaton might be ancestrally connected to the Kerry blue terrier. Kerry blues are known to be territorial with other male dogs and will rarely back down from a fight. This does not guarantee sociability around other dogs. If these dogs are not carefully bred, socialized early on, as well as consistently trained well and given plenty of exercise, they have a tendency toward becoming a bit snappy. I have more clients with wheaton terrier problems than I care to admit.

The Dog of the Moment

In the sixties it was the old English sheepdog and the dalmatian. In the seventies it was the Irish setter and the Saint Bernard. In the eighties it was the Akita and the rottweiler, and, let's not forget those popular nineties dogs—the American pit bull terrier (pit bull), the Jack Russell terrier, and the Border collie. "Dogs of the moment" are dog breeds that come into fashion (via movies, print ads, and television) at any given time, and they often fall prey to many behavioral and physical changes due to supply-and-demand breeding. There are many standards and ethics for dog breeding but no laws that say only nice, healthy dogs can be reproduced.

I read a recent article in a fashion magazine that named the weimaraner as the "dog of the moment" because "the color gray is in." I shuddered at the thought of all those weimaraners walking down Rodeo Drive perfectly suited to their owners' clothing. Dogs of the moment may look great standing next to you but, unfortunately, they must also match your lifestyle and you theirs. Careless breeding practices (due to supply and demand) can slap a monstrous reputation on an otherwise wonderful breed— a reputation that follows them for years to come.

Understanding the limitations of the breed of dog you ultimately choose will only serve to help you live with this dog. If you can't imagine yourself delivering a leash correction for fear you will hurt your dog, make sure you don't get a dog that can pull your body weight. Instead, choose a dog that comfortably keeps you in tow—but will not tow you over. By the same token, if you know yourself well enough to admit that even bossing a dog around makes you squeamish, don't choose a strong-willed breed; they will not be at all squeamish about pushing you around.

If you find a certain breed's personality as well as physical traits desirable and you can provide the appropriate environment for this dog, you will more than likely do well living with it. Because we all have different reasons for wanting to live with a dog and an even greater variety of living situations that the dog must fit into, finding the right breed can be daunting. Here are a few suggestions.

If you are planning to or already have children, these breeds generally do well in a family atmosphere:

- golden retriever
- Labrador retriever
- bichon frise
- Boston terrier
- wire fox terrier
- keeshond
- miniature schnauzer
- Samoyed
- Portuguese water dog
- standard poodle
- Newfoundland
- English setter

If you are looking for a dog that will adapt to city as well as country living, you might have a closer look at these breeds:

- dachshund
- English toy spaniel
- Boston terrier
- miniature schnauzer
- borzoi
- affenpinscher
- Norwich terrier
- cairn terrier
- Italian greyhound
- American cocker spaniel

If you prefer a dog that does not necessarily enjoy being fawned on but instead like living with a dog that has a tendency toward being independent, do a bit of research on these breeds:

- chow chow
- Afghan hound
- briard
- Siberian husky
- basenji
- saluki

In a household with adults or older children (a household that might be inclined to spoil a dog rotten), the following breeds are a good choice:

- silky terrier
- Maltese
- Pekingese
- Chihuahua
- Italian greyhound
- Yorkshire terrier
- shih tzu
- papillon
- French bulldog

If you are athletic and plan to include your dog in your daily exercise routine these dogs have the energy to keep up:

- Irish setter
- smooth fox terrier
- Portuguese water dog
- Airedale terrier
- standard schnauzer
- Chesapeake Bay retriever

If you are in the market for a lapdog, choose a toy breed that enjoys being pampered. If you are looking for a dog who would make a great soul mate for the not-so-weak in spirit, terriers are the mighty dogs of the dog world and will happily take on a challenge ten times their size. But, if you have children running around who might not enjoy being chased like moving targets, steer clear of the terrier family. If you have children who are too young to respect a dog's threshold of pain, don't get a small-boned, fragile dog. The list goes on and on and your choices are limited only by the boundaries of your lifestyle; respecting those boundaries should be your top priority when choosing a dog.

Nonetheless, the bottom line is still the same. The more information you have about any dog, secondhand or puppy, the easier it will be to understand that dog's overall and ultimate behavior. Doing your homework and asking others about the positive and negative experiences they have had with their specific breed of dog, or finding out what details you can about an individual dog's past experiences, will always pay for itself in the end.

You've Got Male

One last factor to consider when shopping for your canine companion is gender preference. Many people have a built-in predilection for gender while others struggle with this option. The choice is ultimately an individual one, but the fact is that with all species, distinct differences between the two sexes exist.

To begin with, male dogs are larger than females and, depending on the breed you choose, difference in body size between genders can vary as much as twenty-five pounds. Size aside, male dogs can be more aggressive, more likely to mark objects with urine (for ownership purposes), more likely to roam, and, yes, more likely to mount other dogs (for sexual satisfaction and to show dominance) and sometimes whatever else they can successfully attach themselves to. This is not always a pretty picture. On the other hand, they are also wonderfully silly and can often be more playful than their female counterparts.

If you do choose a male dog but want to lessen your boy's need to roam, and maybe even curb his amorous nature or his prizefighting personality, try neutering him. Research has shown that removing the testosterone level from your male dog's body can have tremendously calming effects on his libido as well as his adventurous side. Men, however (not male dogs), seem to have a real problem with this issue. It undoubtedly has something to do with "male identification." I know more men, including my own husband, who feel the pain of removing a dog's testicles a lot more than the dog actually does. For this reason alone, many male dogs in need of a little relaxation and peace of mind instead spend their lives looking for love in all the wrong places because their male caretakers are having trouble letting go of the ball—so to speak.

Female dogs, on the other hand, are more likely to stay close to home and are generally easier to housebreak. They are usually more focused on their human families and therefore sometimes easier to train. They come into season, or heat, an average of two times a year for approximately three weeks at a time. It can be messy and bothersome but neutering (spaying) your female will eliminate that problem altogether. Research has also shown that spaying the female dog eliminates the risk of mammary cancer as well as some uterine infections. At any rate, there are far too many unwanted dogs in the world as it is and, for that reason alone, neutering your dog, regardless of its sex, is always more prudent than not.

So there you have it. The choices are great and the options are many. But whatever you choose—male or female, Newfoundland or Pomeranian—do your homework first because, even in the dog world, men are from Mars and women are from Venus.

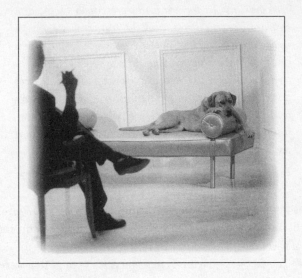

Chapter 11

Is There a Doctor in the House?

What to Do When Your Dog Is Behaving Badly

Spanky, a silky terrier, was a behavioral nightmare and created all kinds of problems for his people. To begin with, he chased the children all over the house. To make matters even worse, whenever the children stopped running from him, he would nip at their feet until the running started all over again. Whenever he wasn't running, he was digging at the floorboards. He rarely slept. Instead, he paced the floors night after night checking to see that each family member was safely asleep in his or her respective bed.

Spanky's veterinarian suggested a trainer. Spanky's

trainer suggested a behaviorist, and Spanky's behav-
iorist diagnosed Spanky with a classic case of separa-
tion anxiety. The behaviorist consulted with the
veterinarian. The veterinarian prescribed Clomicalm
(an antianxiety drug), and the trainer visits once a
week. After months of therapy, thousands of dollars,
and not much progress, Spanky's people decided they
could no longer live with Spanky. Spanky now lives
on a farm in upstate New York. He chases squirrels
and digs for field mice by day and sleeps quite peace-
fully at night. Spanky no longer has any behavioral
problems.

How does one distinguish normal canine behavior from problematic canine behavior? Is your dog having difficulty with his daily life, thus showing signs of psychological trauma? Or is he just behaving like the dog that he actually is? The fact is, behavioral characteristics in dogs that were thought to be desirable just a short century ago are the same characteristics that are often considered undesirable in today's latchkey dog. The protective instinct, physical stamina, and keen hunting skills were all characteristics of the canine that helped to ensure the very survival of the species. Today, however, we regard those same characteristics as aggressive, high-strung, and destructive. Is it the dog who has become unreasonable or simply the parameters within which we expect the dog to live?

This conflict simply amplifies the fact that it is up to dog-loving people to adjust and readjust their "canine-specific" living arrangements. Without some changes, these behavioral "problems" (that were all but nonexistent in the average dog just a few decades ago) will persist, and even worsen. As we've discussed, our options are many: day care for the lonely dog, dog walking for the sedentary dog, training for the unruly dog, massage therapy for the sensitive dog, and psychotropic medications for the anxious dog. While some of these options may be luxuries, others have become downright necessities.

Imagine that your dog suddenly exhibits, or over a period of time develops, troubling behavioral problems. How do you determine what or who is the cause? What should you do and where should you go for help? With a list of professional options as long as the yellow pages itself, the prospect of where to begin can be confusing. Many factors come into play when analyzing a dog's behavior and even more when diagnosing it. If you live with a dog, determining the cause of your dog's behavioral issues—or even determining if your dog has behavioral issues at all—is imperative. However, where does one begin on this road of good intentions?

To Thine Own Self Be True

As a woman, a dog trainer, and a mother, my life experience has proved time and again that the best place to start is with yourself. Trust your instincts. More often than not they are correct. Regardless of your gender, if you have a feeling that something is not right with your dog, the chances are good that something is not right with your dog. You live with your dog, so who better than you to make the initial diagnosis that something is amiss? You are often the only one in a position to recognize the need for concern and, possibly, help. Don't wait until your dog is in the throes of a full-blown problem to admit that you suspected something might have been wrong from the very beginning. If you do suspect that your dog might have a behavioral problem, the first step should always be an appointment with your veterinarian.

Doctor, Doctor

Dogs who behave oddly often have some physiological problem that precipitates their actions. Before attempting to modify any dog's behavior, it must first be determined whether or not the dog is physically sound. Assuming that you have chosen a practitioner whom you trust and respect, your veterinarian is the only one to make this determination.

Because studies have shown that there is a direct connection between physical and mental health in animals, more veterinary schools are now offering residency programs in animal behavior. Because behavior and physical well-being go hand in hand, choosing a veterinarian whose training background includes an interest in behavior can be the difference between a decent doctor and a priceless one.

Feel free to question any method that you either disagree or feel uncomfortable with. Some of us seem to need permission for this. If you are even slightly doubtful about a specific procedure, you owe it to your-self—and your dog—to question away.

Don't be too quick to call a trainer (there's time for that later) before you have discussed even the smallest detail of behavior with your dog's doctor. Sometimes a simple blood test is all it takes to reveal the underlying culprit behind unusual behavior.

The Prince and the Pomeranian

About two years ago, I got a call from a man named Marcus who had just picked up a Pomeranian puppy from a breeder in Massachusetts. He named the puppy Pom and brought her to his vet for an examination where, with the exception of a common parasite, the dog was given a clean bill of health. As Marcus had never owned a dog before, his vet recommended that he enlist the help of a professional trainer and he got my number from a friend.

When I met Pom she was thirteen weeks old. On our initial visit I noticed that the puppy was more timid than a Pomeranian should gen-erally be. I brought this to Marcus's attention and he mentioned that the breeder had not spent very much time socializing the puppies. This, I thought, was definitely the reason for Pom's shy demeanor. We began basic obedience training (which always helps to build communication skills and confidence in dogs) and I felt certain that we could bring this puppy out of her shell in no time.

During my second visit (which was approximately two weeks later), Marcus told me that, in spite of the obedience lessons and his efforts to incorporate Pom into her new family, he had not been terribly success-ful. He also mentioned that about three days after our last meeting, the puppy had fallen from a chair in the living room. Pom did not appear injured at all but, instead, slightly off balance. Marcus had suspected that something was wrong, but because Pom had been to the veterinarian just days before, he decided to wait for their next regularly scheduled appointment to bring the episode to the doctor's attention. I advised against waiting and instead told Marcus to trust his instincts and call the vet as soon as possible.

After examining Pom again (only this time armed with more than just the general appearance of the puppy), the veterinarian ran further tests and found that Pom had a metabolic disorder called a liver shunt. With the help of medication and a prescribed change in diet, in a very short time Pom was like a new dog. Her balance seemed to have been restored to normal and the timid behavior had all but disappeared. In fact, Pom has now matured into one of the most social, outgoing dogs I have had the pleasure to know.

This is just one example of an illness that, left unchecked, could have had potentially life-threatening results for a dog. Without the necessary, detailed information that your veterinarian can get only from you, a doctor's hands are often tied when attempting to diagnose a dog's medical or behavioral problems. Trusting your own instincts does not require a professional background in medicine, but rather a bit of confidence in your own judgment.

Dr. Nicholas Dodman, veterinarian and author of *Dogs Behaving Badly*, devotes an entire chapter of the book to the physiological causes of behavioral problems in dogs. The list includes hormonal disturbances (hypothyroidism), partial seizures, infectious diseases (rabies), metabolic disorders (kidney and liver diseases) and central nervous system problems (tumors, cysts, etc.), trauma (head trauma) problems, congenital problems (hydrocephalus), and allergies. Dr. Dodman explains that hormonal disturbances alone might possibly affect six of the seven dog-breed groups recognized by the American Kennel Club.

Aside from recognizing that there are scores of physiological causes for canine behavioral dilemmas, there are also many behavioral dilemmas that can now be treated with various pharmacologic agents. As discussed earlier, these drugs should be prescribed by and used only under the care of a licensed veterinarian who is familiar with their use in connection with animal behavior.

I work with a wonderful group of veterinarians on the east side of Manhattan called the Center for Veterinary Care. Drs. Paul Schwartz and

Gene Solomon head up the Center for Veterinary Care and they insist on taking the time to discuss the dogs they send to me for training. Even something as simple as a change in diet, which I feel might help aid in eliminating canine behavioral problems, should be overseen and ultimately decided between a dog's owner and the veterinarian. It is imperative to discuss mind and body connections in order to be certain that a potentially dangerous physical condition not be overlooked.

So, if your dog is behaving in an unusual fashion, or you suspect that something might be amiss, remember to trust your instincts first and then call the veterinarian. The doctor should always, and without exception, be the starting point.

Finding the right veterinarian is only one step in this process. When treating behavioral disorders such as separation anxiety, obsessive compulsive disorders, and some aggressive behavior (to mention a few), a veterinarian must be skilled in the uses of several medications as they relate specifically to behavioral problems. Finding the right drug is, unfortunately, only one factor in the equation. Teaming the right drug with the proper dosage is the answer. This can sometimes take several weeks—if not months—and your patience, along with your veterinarian's knowledge in this arena, can be the only winning ticket.

You Ain't Nothin' but a Hound Dog

Aladdin, a four-year-old Afghan hound, lived with his people, Alex and Robert, in New York City. Aladdin had always been a bit aloof (as Afghans can be) but was, for the most part, a lovely, well-balanced dog. Alex and Robert had recently moved to New York City from a quiet suburb in Houston and there had, of course, been an adjustment period for the entire family. Aladdin, however, was having an unusually hard time accepting his new life as a "city dog."

Walking on the crowded, noisy streets seemed more than this pensive canine character could bear. He began to urinate in the lobby of their apartment building and then refuse to go outside altogether. He also began to scratch at the floor near the front door whenever Alex and Robert left him at home. Alex got permission from the "powers that be" in their building to temporarily walk Aladdin on the roof garden so she, too, could avoid going outside with her dog, but did not know what to do about the scratching behavior. Because it was unrealistic to think that Aladdin could spend the remainder of his life between their apartment and the roof garden, and destroying the apartment was just not acceptable, Alex asked around about behaviorists and trainers and decided to start with me. The dog had, in fact, been to see his veterinarian first, who had found nothing apparently wrong with him. After witnessing the dog's behavior, I concluded that Aladdin might be suffering from separation anxiety, due in part to his new surroundings and in part to the change in the family's routine.

Weeks of obedience and behavioral-modification training proved effective, but only up to a point. Then I remembered something I had read in Nicholas Dodman's first book *The Dog Who Loved Too Much* about Afghan hounds sometimes having hormonal disturbances that can, in fact, dramatically affect their behavior. I phoned Dr. Dodman at Tufts University Veterinary School and asked for some advice about Aladdin. He recommended that the dog's vet do a thyroid hormone level test. To everyone's surprise (and relief), Aladdin did, in fact, have a hypothyroid condition.

Shortly after incorporating thyroid medication into the roster of his existing routine of daily training (through basic obedience), the dog began to make remarkable strides. Because he no longer had a problem walking the streets of New York, he got plenty of exercise. So much, in fact, that he was just too tired to do anything but rest when his people were not at home. Although this process took longer than Alex and Robert had anticipated, the result was well worth the team effort—and I stress *team*. Thank you, Dr. Dodman.

Certain behavioral problems, whether linked directly or indirectly to a physical source, are best and sometimes only solved with the help of a behaviorist or a professional trainer. Where a condition of hypothyroidism might well be cured with medication, in Aladdin's case, and in many other situations, a good many of these prescriptions must be administered in conjunction with behavioral modification to be totally effective. With regard to canine-specific behavioral problems, whether physical or emotional, if medication is involved, training and medication must go hand in hand. For instance, if a dog is exhibiting aggressive behavior, your veterinarian might prescribe medication only during a period of modification with a professional behaviorist or trainer. If a behavior goes unchecked long enough to become habitual, regardless of its source, a medication alone might very well be useless without some retraining for the owner as well as the dog.

The Princess and the Pea

Heidi was a six-year-old German shepherd that had been snarling at her owners, Ron and Cynthia, for about nine months. It only happened when they attempted to pet her anywhere near her face but lately it seemed to be happening more often than usual. The behavior was even more disturbing because Cynthia had just given birth to their first child. Because Heidi's snarling started just about the time Cynthia became pregnant, she and Ron thought the behavior must have had something to do with the pregnancy and they became afraid their dog might hurt their baby.

Heidi had been a spoiled "first-child" dog, so being jealous of her new sibling didn't seem a far-fetched prospect. Nonetheless, a trip to the vet for a second opinion couldn't hurt. The veterinarian discovered a painful abscess in the dog's ear canal and drained it immediately. Medication was prescribed to prevent infection, and Cynthia and Ron took their dog home, enormously relieved that their concerns were now over. But Heidi's behavioral problems were far from over.

Apparently, over the nine-month period that the dog was in physical pain, she had become habitually fearful of anyone coming anywhere near her head. Removing the source of the pain had, unfortunately, not removed the habit of being fearful. Because an antibiotic salve had to be applied to the dog's ear, avoiding contact with her head was now impossible. A second discussion with the veterinarian was necessary.

The vet recommended that Heidi be given a mild sedative during the course of antibiotics to ease her stress. At the same time, Cynthia and Ron worked with me to desensitize the dog from its fears. This was done with a food reward anytime anyone went anywhere near the dog's head. Several times a day, Cynthia or Ron would give Heidi a treat while touching her gently on the face. Eventually they could administer the medication while giving the dog the treat reward. In a fairly short period of time, the dog was weaned off the sedative, and because she was now accustomed to a reward (instead of pain) when someone came near her, she began to relax and enjoy the physical contact.

I call this "habitual behavioral backlash," and it is more common than some people might think. When a behavior is repeated often over a period of time, especially when due to a legitimate stimulus, simply removing the stimulus does not necessarily remove the behavior. Behavioral problems in dogs are often multidimensional, and a good veterinarian as well as a good trainer or behaviorist must also be a good detective, peeling away the layers of a problem in order to successfully solve the whole problem.

The moral of this story—simply removing the pea from the bottom of the mattress will not necessarily cure the princess' insomnia.

Trainers, Trainers, Everywhere

Whether you choose a licensed animal behaviorist or a professional dog trainer to modify your dog's behavior, personal recommendation is the best place to start when exercising your options. Whether you live in a metropolis or a remote suburb, your veterinarian should have some recommendations for trainers as well as behaviorists. Also, never hesitate to ask for a recommendation from someone who already has a well-behaved dog. Because dog trainers do not necessarily have to have any formal training to call themselves dog trainers, and no licensing is required in this vast field, a trainer's success rate alone speaks volumes.

Personality is also a key factor in choosing a trainer for you and your dog. If the individual personalities of your family and your dog do not mix with that of the professional who is helping you, you will not be getting your money's worth. Simply find another trainer. And any trainer who tells you it's "their way" or "no way" is waving their own red flag. Good dog trainers can be skilled in a variety of techniques and no one person should claim to have all the answers. The success of any training method is a collective effort between dog, family, and trainer. If the advice you are being given makes you uncomfortable, that should be a red flag as well.

The success of the overall effort ultimately depends on the owner's comfort level with the professional. Some of the best dog trainers I know are great with dogs but horrible with people. If a trainer comes into your home and works magic with your dog, but excludes you from the equation—unless that trainer agrees to move in with you and solve any future problems—the result will not be a successfully trained dog. Any dog trainer can and should be able to train your dog—after all, that is what we do. The real art is in training you to train your dog. Because the ultimate responsibility of training falls on the people who live with the dog, choosing an effective people trainer is even more important than choosing a great dog trainer. Again, I strongly encourage asking other dog owners or dog professionals who have had success with a particular trainer or behaviorist for a personal recommendation. Such a reference can be far better than a first-class résumé.

Group Therapy

If it's a group class you're looking for (and I strongly recommend that all dogs have, at the very least, some group instruction), be sure to check out the class without your dog before signing up. If the atmosphere is comfortable as well as productive, and you find yourself wishing you were already a part of the activity you are observing, sign away. Group classes require a skilled trainer who not only can juggle the ball between many dogs and their owners but also can give some individual attention when needed. Every dog and owner team works at a different pace and it is the job of the instructor to make each and every team feel good about their individual progress. Laughter, believe it or not, is another essential part of this mix. Because dogs respond far more quickly to pleasure than stress, bringing levity to this and any other learning process makes all the difference when training a dog.

Nonetheless, whoever you decide to use, behaviorist or trainer, individual instruction or group, be sure to ask for references and take the time to check them out. It can save you a lot of time and aggravation— not to mention money.

Chow Time

Believe it or not, even dogs have eating disorders. Most of them do not stem from what we feed our dogs but, instead, the way we feed them. Food represents many things to animals. Wild animals of all species simply eat to stay alive, while domesticated animals have learned to eat for the sheer pleasure of it. It is this eating for pleasure—combined with some other rituals associated with the art of eating—that contributes to big canine behavioral problems.

Since we (the people) are in charge of doling out the food, we obviously have a hand in fostering (or creating) many of these behavioral issues. First, let's discuss what motivates us to feed our dogs. Love, guilt, and bribery are just a few impulses that cause us to reach for the food bag. Nothing soothes the guilt of daily abandonment like a nice bowl of food—right? Why then are so many of our dogs leaving those bowls of food untouched day after day, while others are painstakingly dragging pieces out of the dish only to hide them under the coffee table, and still others growling if we even come near them while they are eating? It has far less to do with the menu and much more to do with the service.

One of the most significant rituals of pack living is mealtime. To a dog, a meal (or any food, for that matter) signals a time when the group comes together to rejoice in the spoils of the hunt. Each time the pack eats, the hierarchy of the group is reinforced by the strongest eating first and so on down the line. Some dogs who are not required to perform a task for their food begin to automatically perceive themselves as high-ranking pack members who are "entitled" to what they eat. Consequently, these dogs have a tendency to become possessive and maybe even aggressive later on in life. Others, who are required to eat alone (because we simply cannot stay home), become confused about their status in the pack and eventually insecure about eating altogether. These insecure dogs won't eat unless someone is home or even in the same room with them. It's difficult to believe that the way you feed your dog might just be undermining (or perhaps overinflating) his self-esteem, therefore altering his overall behavior, but it does. If your dog is constantly dining alone or never required to pick up the tab, something behavioral is eventually bound to give.

Food for Thought

Pal was a four-year-old bearded collie who lived with his family, Robert and Callie and their two children, on a farm in southern Connecticut. For the first year of his life, Pal was friendly, obedient, and affectionate toward everyone around him. The couple began obedience training him when he was just seven weeks old and had never had any real problems with him. That is, not until he began stealing table scraps from the kitchen floor and growling at anyone who tried to challenge him.

Friends of Callie and Robert's who were clients of mine asked if I could be of any help with Pal, so I packed up my car and headed to Connecticut. Callie and Robert's farm was the perfect setting for any dog. Plenty of room to run, at least one family member around all the time, and farm animals galore, this was every herding dog's dream. I knew instantly that neither a lack of exercise nor a lack of companionship was to blame for the behavioral problems of this dog.

Aggressive canine behavior can be blamed on several things. Genetics often plays a role when dominance rears its ugly head. Physical illness, territoriality, and predatory factors also come in to play. Sometimes, however, dominance is fostered by the environment in which a dog spends its time (see chapter 5, "Rover Rage"). Such was the case with Pal.

Callie, Robert, and I began our meeting by discussing Pal's history. Neighbors owned both of Pal's parents and they assured me that both mother and father were as sweet as sugar. Pal's veterinarian had already checked him out from head to toe and had ruled out any physical cause for the behavior. That left us with one other avenue to explore—determining just how much was required of this dog as a working member of the pack.

Callie gave me a brief overview of the household dynamic. Each human member of the family had set chores each day and was required to do them before he or she could even consider free time. Before breakfast the children fed the animals (Pal included) and cleaned up their respective rooms. Mom and Dad milked the cows and cleaned out the stalls. Once the morning chores were completed, the family sat down to a quick breakfast and then went their separate ways for the day.

Nobody gave the routine a second thought until the day one of the kids dropped a piece of food on the floor. When he reached down to pick it up, Pal (who was also reaching for the food) growled and started to snap. Before that morning, Pal had never been aggressive about anything. He was not a thief by nature, nor had he ever challenged anyone in the house about anything. After that morning, however, Pal began stealing eggs out of the chicken coop, laundry out of the laundry basket (he had a preference for undergarments), and scraps of food that had been dropped on the kitchen floor.

The first question I asked was, "*Who* feeds the dog?" Callie and Robert's ten-year-old son proudly chimed in that the job was his. My next question was, "*How* did he feed the dog?" The boy explained that he filled the bowl while Pal danced around, waiting to eat. After putting the bowl down, the boy went out to do the rest of his chores as the dog charged in to consume his food. This routine, I explained, was more than likely the cause of the problem. Pal, it seemed, was the only family (or pack) member who was not required to perform any chores for his food. Even the children pitched in and worked for their food. Being the only family member exempt from this responsibility would be likely to make any living creature think he was king.

I explained how important it was for a dog to "work for a living," and that without this "work" dogs begin to think they are entitled not only to the food, but to just about anything else they might want. By failing to require the dog to perform any task for his meals, the family had inadvertently taught their dog that he was the highest ranking member of their pack, entitled to take whatever he wanted, whenever he wanted it. Pal's belief that he was "top dog" explained his aggressive behavior around fallen table scraps as well as his theft of eggs from the chicken coop. It was, without a doubt, time to dethrone the king—or, in this case, the dog.

I suggested a simple change in the family's routine. Instead of feeding Pal before the rest of the chores were done, the chores were to be done first. Pal could wait. When the family was ready to sit down to breakfast, Pal's breakfast could be prepared, too. Just before the dog's meal was to be served, he was to be commanded to "sit" and "stay." After a moment or so, he could be released from the "stay" and allowed to eat. Sitting and staying would be the dog's "chores" and the meal would be his reward. This would let Pal know that he was not royalty, but was instead a member of the working class. Even more important, it would teach him that he was not "entitled" to anything. From then on, he was to work for a living like everybody else in the house.

After about a week into Pal's new routine, which also included the family deliberately dropping food on the floor and leaving undergarments out around the house, and telling the dog to "leave it" whenever he approached them, Robert phoned me with a progress report. It seemed the laundry was no longer being sorted by the dog and the chicken coop was virtually collie-free. Robert said that he and Callie observed that Pal seemed happier now that something was expected of him. I confirmed that the chances were good that he was much happier. A successful coup indeed. As much as I would have loved another visit to Robert and Callie's, it was clear that there was no longer any need for a dog trainer down on that farm.

Dogs who are not required to perform at least some task for their food are prone to developing all kinds of behavioral problems. Aggression is just one example of such problems. Some dogs who see food as a gift eventually lose interest in food altogether. These dogs are often required to eat alone because we feed them a few moments before we head out the door. Without the presence of the pack to complete the mealtime ritual, mealtime becomes the signal that the dog is about to be left behind. Food then becomes the source of stress and stress becomes the source of yet another behavioral avalanche.

Believe it or not, dogs will eat when and if they are hungry. Skipping a meal is not necessarily the end of the world, but if your dog ignores his food on a regular basis, or will eat only when you stand nearby and coax him to, or leaves the food untouched all day only to charge for it ravenously when you arrive home at night, the chances are that your dog is not physically sick, but instead emotionally overwrought. Putting the dog to work at mealtime often corrects these "food issues."

If your dog is a disinterested or picky eater, try feeding him his next meal—or even his next treat—as payment for a task. Remember, a simple "sit" will do. If the food is a reward instead of a gift or a representation of your love, the dog will really appreciate the earned meal and you will really appreciate his resulting cooperation.

Nutrition and exercise also play an important role in your dog's overall well-being. Dogs who are sedentary for a good portion of the day must be allowed to expend their stored-up energy somehow. If your dog's diet is either too high in protein or too high in calories, coupled with little or no exercise, his behavior will eventually begin to reflect that of an athlete who's been indefinitely suspended from his sport. Unpredictable bursts of obnoxious energy, as well as general nervous behavior, are just two of the major symptoms of the sedentary dog.

Every day, without exception, your dog needs to rid his body of the tension that will grip his muscles if he is not allowed or required to burn energy through exercise. Seventy-five percent of all canine behavioral issues that I deal with could actually be averted or, at the very least, minimized with the help of sufficient daily movement. Even a short-term sabbatical from an exercise routine can have a profound effect on the average dog's personality.

So, if you're worried because your dog is shooting around like a rocket just launched into space, don't be. Instead, take the dog for a good long aerobic walk (every day) or find a field and play fetch until your dog can fetch no more. Many behavioral problems are solved with a daily dose of exercise. You know the adage—"A tired dog is a good dog." Thankfully, no other medicine is needed here.

Nothing to Sneeze At

If your dog continually scratches himself, is hyperactive, or obsessively licks his own paws (or perhaps even you), it's time to dial the doctor once more. Some believe that certain behavioral dilemmas in dogs stem from the foods they eat. Whether it is a natural ingredient (such as corn) or a chemical additive (such as ethoxyquin) in your dog's food that's causing the problem, dogs, like people, do suffer from allergies, and allergies can, in fact, affect behavior.

If you have been diligent about training, have made certain to exercise the dog daily as well as to properly socialize him to the outside world and obsessive or unusual behavior persists, ask the vet to look into allergies. Some might say it's a long shot, but I say that allergies are nothing to sneeze at.

What's in a Breed?

If you want to save yourself an arm and a leg in expensive, often time-consuming training and medical alternatives, it always helps to know your own dog's specific breed traits before assuming that something is actually wrong with your dog's behavior. Different breeds of dogs have been bred, for centuries, to behave in a certain way. As mentioned before, the habit of terriers (who have been deliberately bred to chase moving things on the ground) to chase and nip at moving feet is not a behavioral problem, but rather a natural trait of the breed.

Just as retrievers have been purposefully bred to carry things in their mouths, so, too, have herding dogs been bred to be adept at keeping things in nice, tight groups. So, if your retriever is constantly carrying around your socks or forever chewing on sticks, the chances are that there's nothing wrong with your retriever. He's just being—you guessed it—a retriever. And, by the same token, if your herding dog begins to exhibit signs of separation anxiety, it's probably because he is, in fact, anxious about the group, or any group, for that matter, breaking up and going in separate directions. He is, after all, a herding dog.

Many who worry about what they believe are their dog's specific personality disorders are actually worrying about behavior that, while specific to the breed, is perfectly normal. And take my word for it—trying to change a natural breed trait can take a lifetime.

The responsibility of recognizing whether or not a dog has a behavioral problem belongs, without question, with his owners. Since behavioral problems can run the gamut from aggression to agoraphobia (abnormal fear of being in open spaces), knowing when to be alarmed and when to be accepting can have a profound effect on your dog's behavior and, therefore, on your relationship with your dog.

With so many new problems for our modern dogs to deal with, the necessity for professional help has dramatically increased. But, as your dog's caretaker, do not discount the importance that you play. While dogs who suddenly develop a new set of behaviors may well need professional help to get back on track, examining both your lifestyle as well as your relationship with your dog can often give you valuable clues as to the cause of the behavior. By taking all of this into consideration, you really are being your own dog's best friend, which is the next best thing to having a doctor in the house.

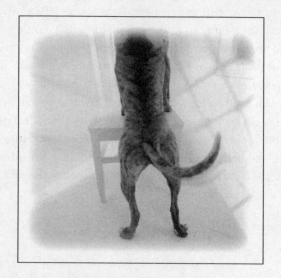

Chapter 12

Wag the Dog

Creating Solutions

Instead of spending so much time and energy trying to get your dog to wag his tail, why not just pick up the dog and shake him until his tail starts to wag?

With the topic of dog behavior becoming as hot as that of alternative medicine, finding a way to get your dog to "comply" has become more a matter of individual style than right or wrong. But whatever your style—when it comes to giving orders—the fact remains that many dog owners are afraid of upsetting their dogs.

But what if (with a bit of creative thinking on your part) training your dog could be a pleasurable experience for you—and the dog? I call this alternative training "wag the dog" and it is about finding a way to get your dog to do what *you* say while giving the dog what *he* wants—a way to make *you* happy.

Zippity Do Da

Zippity, the mutt, likes to sleep in bed with his owner, Ben. But Ben doesn't like it when he gets into bed and the dog is already there, asleep on his pillow. It's not that he minds the dog in the bed, he just minds that the dog has claimed his side of the bed. Every evening, it's the same routine. Ben goes to bed and finds Zippity already settled in for the night. The problem starts when Ben tries to move Zippity off the pillow. This otherwise seemingly good-natured dog snarls and bares his teeth. Not wanting to get bitten by his own dog, Ben quickly backs away and begrudgingly sleeps on the other side of the bed. In other words, Zippity acts and Ben reacts. But once Ben became aware that his response to his dog's behavior was actually reinforcing it, the man was more than ready to take a new tack.

Their new routine began by Ben refusing to allow the dog on the bed at all (by gently pushing him "off" until Zippity got the picture) unless the dog was actually given a "command" to jump up. So, if the dog wanted to go on the bed, he would have to wait to be invited onto the bed. When Ben was ready to turn in, he would call Zippity, who was by that time asleep on the floor (remember, he's not allowed on the bed unless invited) and command him to "come" and "wait." Ben would then get in bed, claim his spot, and command Zippity to jump on the bed. Everybody's happy, right?

The laws of physics have taught us that for every action, there is a reaction. Why would we think our interaction with our dogs would be any different? If you can teach your dog to "act" based on how you "react" (and not the other way around), then you won't have to spend so much time making the dog happy—the dog will start thinking about how to make you happy (something the dog actually prefers anyway).

If you show the dog the behavior you expect from him, he will do it simply because your reaction is one of pleasure and, believe it or not, if you are pleased with your dog for a job well done, your dog is going to be pleased with himself. Thereafter, for the sheer pleasure of it, he will repeat the behavior that makes you happy.

Someone recently asked me if I could recommend any new or interesting activities for her dog. This woman was away all day and worried that, left alone at home, her dog might be bored. I answered that I thought it much more important that she focus on what the dog was doing when the woman was at home (i.e., requiring the dog to follow several simple obedience commands). This way, when the dog was at home alone, he would spend the day resting. Having worked (for the woman) all evening, the dog would actually be grateful for the "time off." See what I mean . . . there's more than one way to wag the dog.

Wagging the dog is a lot like marketing a new product. Have you ever wondered why we buy so many things that we might otherwise ignore if they were just sitting on the shelves in generic wrappers? We are drawn to them because they are presented in attractive packages. The packaging attracts us and, if the products taste or feel good enough, we try them again and again. Once we are "sold" on these products, they become staples in our daily diet and as natural a part of our daily routine as breathing.

If dog training and behavioral modification were approached in much the same way, our dogs would be drawn or attracted to doing things our way and, eventually, our way would become a part of their behavioral diet. Being creative not only makes behavioral modification and dog training fun, it opens up an entire world of possibilities for man, woman, and dog. The concept is simple: Your desire for the dog to do something is the product, and, if you're going to sell it to your dog, you'll need to wrap it in a package your dog can understand.

If your dog does not "come" when you call, make the act of "coming to you" more attractive and your dog will want to come—whenever you call. If your dog is begging for food at the table, simply teach your dog (through reward) what you expect by making "down-stay" a more attractive proposition than begging at the table. Once you do this, the begging will cease. If your dog is not eating his meals, simply make his meals a reward or a payment (via a basic obedience command) for a job well done, and his appetite should quickly change from finicky to famished. There are all kinds of ways to change your dog's behavior and, if you are open to a little creativity, your options are limitless.

From Russia with Love

Dimitri, a borzoi (Russian wolfhound), belongs to Paul and Petra. The pup was given to them when he was eight weeks old as an anniversary gift from their grown children. Both Paul and Petra were thrilled at the prospect of raising this puppy, and although it had been years since a dog had lived with them, they were looking forward to the challenge.

Petra began Dimitri's training as soon as he arrived. The dog learned to "sit," "down," and "stay" very quickly and was housebroken in a reasonably shot period of time. At his own mealtimes, Dimitri learned to sit and stay until he was told he could eat. He was a gentle, good-natured puppy who was fast becoming a well-behaved young dog. Petra and Paul did, however, have a few training hurdles they just could not seem to get over. Dimitri, it seemed, would not come when he was called, had an insatiable urge to chew shoes, and was an impossible nuisance around the dinner table. They called me for some help.

When I arrived, I explained that all dogs are able—if not always willing—students. Just because a dog quickly learns most of his basic obedience commands does not necessarily mean that he is certain about how to respond to all of these orders. More often than not, it is our direction that confuses them, our direction that prompts the undesirable response. For example, if a dog doesn't "come" when he is called, it's probably because the dog isn't sure that's what he is supposed to do. Perhaps you have spent too much time chasing the dog, only to scold him when he finally does decide to come to you. But by scolding the dog in your frustration, you are actually teaching him not to "come" when called. And the same holds true when applied to almost all other obedience dilemmas.

In Dimitri's case, Petra and Paul needed to let their dog know that coming when called is always a good thing, chewing shoes is never a good thing, and doing a "down-stay" while the family was at the dinner table was the only thing. Each issue was to be treated as completely independent of the others. Our first job was to tackle the problem at the dinner table.

We sat down at the table, placed some cheese on our plates, and acted as if it were dinner as usual. Dimitri immediately began to poke his nose into the plates (borzois are very tall dogs) and whine for food. Having seen all that I needed to see, I asked Paul to get Dimitri's leash. Once we'd clipped it on him, I promptly told the dog to "down." He refused. Giving the command was only the first part of the exercise; the second was showing or helping him to do it. I warned Petra and Paul that their dog might not initially like or appreciate the help. I stepped on the leash, just next to the buckle where the collar was attached. Dimitri had little choice but to lie down. Initially, the dog resisted but when he did finally "down," I praised him and gave him one of his chew toys to keep him busy. Once he was relaxed, I put some slack in the leash. If he tried to get up, I again put my foot closer to the buckle and repeated the exercise. Petra and Paul tried the exercise with Dimitri and he quickly caught on to the fact that he was expected to lie down and relax whenever they sat down for dinner. Petra and Paul were learning to wag their dog.

The next problem to tackle was the dog's shoe fetish. Petra had taken to hiding all the shoes in the house so Dimitri would not be tempted to eat them. I explained that in order for the dog to know that they were displeased about his eating their property, they had to let him know their displeasure in the present tense. Because you cannot modify behavior you don't see, this exercise had to be practiced when someone was around. We took several pairs of Petra's and Paul's shoes and scattered them around the living room. We all sat comfortably and waited. It didn't take long for Dimitri to give in to temptation and grab a shoe. I immediately said, "Leave it!" Startled, Dimitri looked at me and promptly dropped the shoe. Instantly, I changed the tone in my voice to one of great pleasure and softly praised Dimitri for dropping the shoe. As a reward for the dog's correct response, I quickly gave Dimitri one of his own toys to chew. Once he tired of his own toy and went back to a shoe, I repeated the "Leave it!," then praised and rewarded him again for dropping the shoe. Paul and Petra practiced this exercise for several minutes until Dimitri had a very clear understanding that shoes were not to be chewed and his own toys were. Putting temptation out in the open (and not in a cupboard) is the only way to help a dog to understand what he can and cannot own.

Now for the "come" command. This is probably the single most important word that your dog can know. If you require nothing else of your dog, coming when called is an absolute must for the safety of the dog as well as the safety of others. As I mentioned earlier, I suspected that Dimitri was not absolutely sure what the word "come" meant.

To further clarify (and perhaps confuse you at the same time), I would like to add that the word "come" is not a necessity in this exercise. Remember that whatever word or phrase you choose, always use it in conjunction with a reward. Whether the reward is food or affection or both, it is the association between the word and the reward that will get your dog's attention. The word(s), whatever they are, must be used consistently by all family members. Even the slightest change will result in a less than perfect result.

I had noticed earlier in our meeting that Petra had a sort of "pet" name for Dimitri. She had used it several times, in almost a whisper tone, whenever he was close enough for the woman to touch him. The nickname was "Dimi," and when she said it she would gently stroke the dog's face in such an endearing way that it instantly relaxed him. I asked her about this and she explained that it was her way of letting the dog know that he was unconditionally loved. This was the opening I was looking for.

I asked Paul to take Dimitri into the kitchen—not by the collar, but by coaxing him away with a bit of food. When Paul and the dog were out of the room, I asked Petra to say "Dimi" two or three times in a row in the same gentle tone she had used earlier. She did, and to her amazement, the dog came running. When he got to her, Petra stroked him affectionately. Dimitri, I explained, had been conditioned to receive affection whenever he heard the pet name "Dimi." Petra had always used it when the dog was already at her side, but she had no idea that she could actually get him to come to her just by saying it. We tried it from several places in the house and then outside in the yard. Each time the dog heard "Dimi," he would come bounding toward Petra for a dose of unconditional love.

Now that Petra and Paul have learned how to wag their dog, the dog not only lies comfortably at their feet at mealtime, he chews his own toys instead of their shoes and he comes when he is called.

The fundamental principles of wagging the dog can be applied to any command or trick that you choose. Let's say (just for the fun of it) that your dog is a habitual thief and you are constantly chasing him around trying to get back what is rightfully yours. Sound familiar? Well, your dog is quickly learning that stealing "your" things is a game that not only wins him a prize but wins him your attention as well. But, if you instead try wagging the dog, you will both end up with what you want— you, an obedient dog, and the dog, success. Here's how you do it.

First and foremost, stop chasing the dog. I know it sounds crazy— the dog does, after all, have something that belongs to you. But, if you, instead of making the pursuit of your belongings a daily game of "catch me if you can," tell him (in the sweetest voice you can muster) what a good dog he is for retrieving whatever it is he has and (in an even sweeter voice) what an amazing dog he is for bringing it and giving it to you, he will then learn that returning your belongings to you is far more pleasant than stealing them. If you have the patience, try this first with some objects that have little meaning for you. You will see that while old habits might die hard, they do eventually die.

Now, if you're a sports fan and are looking for one of those amazing Frisbee-playing dogs, you can actually teach your dog to be one. Though it is true that some dogs are born with natural athletic ability, others can be trained to be athletes. It is, in a way, very much based on the same premise as teaching the "come" command, only this time you'll be using the words "give" and "take." You need to praise your dog for bringing something to you in order to cultivate his "giving" expertise. When the dog has something in his mouth and comes close to you, coax him closer with an almost songlike delivery of the praise by saying "good give."

Once you have the object, give it back to the dog and say "take." If he takes it, say "good take." Repeat this "give" and "take" exercise several times with the dog right in front of you. When you feel the dog has a pretty good idea that "take" means to take the object and "give" means to give the object to you, toss the object a few feet away and say "take." Your dog should go and get the object and that's when you say "good take." Now say "give" and, with any luck, the dog will come to you and give you the object. Eventually, no matter how far you throw the object, if you say "take," the dog will try to get it. If you say "give," the dog will bring it back. Many a canine athlete has been successfully trained this way. Once again, you are merely wagging the dog.

Let's talk about all those dogs that do, for the most part, come when called but only and not until you've raised your voice to such an ear-piercing octave that he—and everyone else within earshot—comes running out of sheer terror. To begin with, stop talking. Again, I know it sounds counterintuitive, but it works. Get yourself a dog whistle, or any other whistle for that matter (the object is less important than the delivery). The point is to settle on something, other than you, that makes a noise, even if it is only discernible to the dog. The sound of the object (like a whistle), however low or loud, never really changes its tone (unlike your voice). Removing emotion when dog training (with the exception of praise) can save you countless embarrassing moments and spares your dog a lot of confusion. This exercise applies the same basic principles as clicker training (a method of training developed in the 1950s by two psychologists/animal trainers named Breland. The Brelands used clickers to reinforce and shape learning by pairing the sound of the clicker with a reward. This conditioned the dog to respond to a specific sound and, as a result, to receive a reward.

To begin: Do this indoors. Take the whistle (if that is your object of choice) and blow it gently. Do it in the same (indoor) room where the dog is so he is initially only required to look at you when you blow it. Now give the dog a small food treat while simultaneously giving voice praise—just for looking your way. Do this for a day or so and begin to coax the dog so close to you that you can pet him as well as praise him (teaching him to "come to you," not to just come near you) before giving the food reward. After a couple of days, start blowing the whistle from another room, requiring the dog to find you first in order to receive the affection and the food. The dog will soon learn that the sound of the whistle means that he must find you (wherever you are) and receive love and food. Once you have achieved the desired level of response indoors, begin to try it outdoors. Simultaneously incorporate the phrase "good come" when you are praising the dog and, should you forget your whistle, the "come" command should get the same result. Most important, you now have a dog that comes when he is called. What could be better? Well, there is one thing: a dog that comes immediately and enthusiastically when called.

If you want to be certain that your dog comes to you with boundless enthusiasm the first time you whistle—and this also applies to those who choose to use their voice for the "come" command—you must learn to praise accordingly. This simply means that you grade the dog in terms of his performance, and the categories being graded are speed and enthusiasm. If you fall all over the dog with love and food every time he saunters over, he will learn that coming in his own good time will win the same reward as coming when you call him. It's like giving someone an A grade for a C performance.

By the same token, if you restrain yourself with the praise and the food rewards, only delivering the "full monty" when he comes roaring to your side the first time he hears the signal, he will learn to come roaring the first time he hears the signal. If you apply the grading system or "praise-according-to-performance" method to all aspects of your relationship with your dog, you will see his overall attention to you increase tenfold in no time. Now you're really learning how to wag the dog.

Even people who have lived with dogs all of their lives but want to try a few new tricks or even break an old habit have found wagging the dog to be the simplest, most pleasant way to get what they want from their dogs. Because so many dog owners are having a hard time telling their latchkey dogs what to do, wag the dog can solve just about any training problem you have—all you need is a little imagination.

The Mirror Trick

A couple of years ago a client of mine named Betsy decided to purchase a petite basset griffon Vendeén. This is an old French breed in the hound family, sometimes affectionately referred to as the PVGV. It had been some years since she had owned a dog and she (as she put it) "had never had a relationship with a dog that hadn't turned out to be a disaster." She was, however, determined not to let that happen to her relationship with her next dog. So determined, in fact, that she decided to hire me to help her train the dog even before she got the dog.

Hiring, or at the very least speaking with, a trainer before you get a dog is actually a very good idea. Learning to avoid a problem is much better than having to learn how to solve one. Anyway, Betsy and I discussed everything from paper training to off-leash training before the puppy ever even stepped foot in the house. When Lily, as Betsy named her, finally moved in, at the ripe old age of twelve weeks, she was not without some already built-in baggage. For all our conversations as dog trainer and dog owner, nothing (not even I) could have prepared Betsy for the one habit this dog already had . . . Lily ate her own feces.

This behavior is called "coprophagy." Whatever drives some puppies to eat their own waste, whether it is a learned behavior (from their mother, who eats her puppies' feces in order to keep the nest clean) or an innate one, most puppies do outgrow the distasteful habit after a few months. Betsy, however, wasn't going to wait a few months, or even a few days for that matter, for her new puppy to outgrow this behavior. She was willing to try anything (short of an exorcism) to rid Lily of her overwhelming desire to eat her own poop.

I explained that short of spiking Lily's food with chili powder or changing her diet altogether (to something less palatable, i.e., with less protein), the best way to be certain that this pup didn't eat her poop was to clean it up before the dog had a chance to. This proved far more easily said than done because Lily didn't like to move her bowels in front of Betsy. Because it is nearly impossible to modify behavior you don't actually witness, Betsy and I were left to figure out some other way to let Lily know that her taste for waste was downright disgusting. Betsy's kitchen (where Lily spent the better portion of her unsupervised hours) was of a long, narrow, galley-type design. It had only one doorway, so if Betsy stood there waiting for Lily to eliminate, the puppy would just wait until Betsy was gone. At the end of the kitchen was the dining room, which led to a foyer that, when you were standing in it, did not have a view of the kitchen. This gave Betsy a brilliant idea.

She placed one of the dining room chairs in the foyer and set a side table next to it. On the side table she put a small dressing mirror and angled it so that (from the seat) she could see directly into the kitchen.

The trick was that the dog could not see the chair, the mirror, or Betsy. Betsy gave Lily her midday meal and left the kitchen. She parked herself on the chair, readjusted the angle of the mirror so that she had a perfect view of the kitchen, and waited. It didn't take long before Lily "had to go" and Betsy was there, waiting in the wings. The very moment the dog went to eat the poop, Betsy rounded the corner and scolded the puppy ("leave it") for what she was about to do. Startled, Lily jumped away from the pile and ran toward Betsy. Betsy opened her arms and greeted her puppy with enthusiasm and lovingly praised her for coming to her.

After a few days of the "mirror trick," Lily was convinced that eating her poop was not worth the scolding she got whenever she went near it. Even when Betsy wasn't home, Lily left the pile on the paper because the pup was now convinced that Betsy would always appear whenever she went near the poop. For this idea alone, Betsy was practically a certified dog wagger. She and Lily have creatively managed to work out just about all of their training issues this way and, consequently, this dog and this woman are rarely at odds.

The mirror trick, or a similar version of it, can be used to solve all sorts of problems. If your dog is stealing food from the kitchen counters or the dining room table, try leaving some "bait" on the counter and hiding behind a wall. If you "set up" the situation first, you have at least a modicum of control. But, if you wait for the dog to spy the hors d'oeuvres on the coffee table while you are greeting your guests at the front door, the chances are that you won't be serving those hors d'oeuvres to your guests and, even worse, the dog won't have learned that stealing food is unacceptable.

Blue Skies

When I was in my twenties, before I was ready to be the mother to my own human children, I had a golden retriever named Blue. Emotionally speaking, he was my firstborn and I loved him as much as I would love my own children. I got him when he was seven weeks old and had decided long before I did so that this dog was going to be the best-trained dog I had ever had. For me, a dog trainer, that should have been an easy task. After all, I already knew (or thought I knew) all there was to know about raising the well-mannered dog. Boy, was I in for a surprise!

Blue was a willing student. I realized, however, when he was still quite young that as much as this dog was learning from me, I was learning even more from him. I taught him a new trick on an average of every three days, whereas he taught me something new about dogs every day. The first thing he taught me was that some dogs do not appreciate physical help when in school. He simply would not allow me to physically help him do anything. If I told him to "sit," he would sit. But if the "sit" was sloppy and I wanted it to be perfect, I would have to figure out how to "fix" him without physically changing his position myself; he simply took offense at being pushed (even gently) around. If I pressed my luck and decided to do it my way, the whole exercise fell apart. I believe Blue was just embarrassed by the prospect of my having to physically fix him. In any case, if this dog and I were going to be a team, *I* was going to have to figure out another way.

I tried several different training techniques, to no avail, and one day while I was working on the "heel" position (when a dog comes around to your left side and automatically sits, his right shoulder lined up with your left knee), Blue leaned (as dogs will do) against my leg. Without thinking, I nudged him with my knee and told him to "straighten out." It happened so fast that neither one of us realized that I had physically helped him. Anyway, he quickly sat up in a perfect, straight sit, in the heel position. I instantly praised him by saying "good straighten out." We were both so excited about the team effort that "straighten out" became a new command. From that day on, whenever Blue needed fixing, whether for a simple sit or a sloppy heel, I just told him to "straighten out" and he would instantly fix himself.

Next came the task of heeling as a walking exercise. Coaxing this dog into position with a leash was the same as physically helping him. So, again, I had to figure out another way. Eye contact was the key. If I could make Blue look at me while we were walking (side by side), he would automatically be in a perfect heel position. When we walked, I praised him only when our eyes made contact and, in no time, Blue learned to look at me whenever and wherever we walked. The result was a dog walking in the perfect heel position.

I was fascinated by the concept of being able to get this dog to do what I wanted, when I wanted, but on his terms. Training him became my most rewarding work. It occurred to me that I could teach him to do anything as long as I took the time to see the world through his eyes first. If he jumped up to greet me (as all dogs will unless they are taught not to), I would quickly bend at the waist and fall, like a building crumbling on him. Because dogs are inherently afraid of things falling out of the sky, he instantly made the connection that staying on the ground was much safer than jumping on me.

As most retrievers do, Blue loved the water. As both my husband's parents and mine have houses near the beach, swimming became a routine activity in Blue's life. He was, it seemed, almost always wet. One of the most annoying things a dog can do is to shake the excess water from his body while he is standing right next to you. Blue was no exception. I thought it might be useful if I could teach him to "shake" his body on command rather than on reflex. On went the thinking cap.

Blue had a rope with a knot at each end and I noticed that he liked to take one end in his mouth and furiously shake the other. I took one end of the bone and gave him the other as if we were going to play tug-of-war. Then I shook my end of the bone while he held on to his end. With great enthusiasm, I said, "Shake, shake." We did this several times a day for a couple of days. Then I gave him the whole bone—placing one of the knots in his mouth—and said, "Shake, shake." To my delight, he shook the bone as he had when we played with it together. I was almost there— but then came the tricky part. After several more days of the two of us shaking the bone together, followed by the dog shaking the bone by himself, I put the bone away and told the dog to shake. I had incorporated a hand signal from the start, knowing it would help once I had eliminated the rope bone from the exercise. At first, he looked at me as if I was crazy. But after a few enthusiastic "Shake!" commands from me, he actually shook—first his head and then his whole body. From that day on, whenever Blue went for a swim or had a bath or walked in the rain, I would tell him to stay, move a reasonably safe distance from him, and then tell him to "shake." Training aside, I saved a hell of a lot of money on dry-cleaning bills.

This wonderful animal proved to be everything I had expected of him and more. He was the kind of dog every friend and stranger admired and every dog lover wishes for. He helped to teach both of my children how to walk by always moving one step farther than they could reach, giving them a reason to take one more step toward him. He taught countless frightened children that there was little need to be frightened of a dog. He hunted like a true gun dog at my husband's side but refused to ever retrieve something as unpalatable as a bloodied bird. I think, as much as he loved to spend the day in the woods, if he had had his druthers, he would rather have hunted tennis balls.

Blue died two days shy of his eighth birthday and every day of his life was a gift to me and my family. He taught me more than I had ever expected to learn from one dog. He taught me the greatest dog-training lesson of my life: He taught me how to wag a dog.

With so many experts telling us what to do and what not to do, the average dog lover is often left reeling. Since all dogs need to be taught what we expect of their behavior, and we as their caretakers seem to be having a rather difficult time telling them what it is that we expect—out of the fear that we might send the wrong message—wag the dog clearly offers solutions that work for the modern dog and owner. Wagging the dog helps you find a way to let your dog know what makes you happy without having to worry about whether the dog thinks you still love him. It's really just dog training with a much needed contemporary spin or, as Mary Poppins put it, "a spoonful of sugar helps the medicine go down."

Conclusion

I must confess that I myself am guilty of many of the indulgences that have contributed to the phenomenon of the latchkey dog. But most of all, I confess to loving dogs. With a résumé that boasts such qualities as loyal, hard-working, forgiving, and loving, who wouldn't love a dog?

But, in an age where time spent at home is at a premium and we are grappling with contemporary, real-life decisions (such as who will go to summer camp—the kids or the dog?), an age in which the most meaningful long-term relationship you've had is not with a mate but with your dog—something that leaves you searching for the line on your tax forms that says "codependent"—is it any wonder that our canines are having difficulty keeping a perspective on reality?

Instead, why not teach your dog what you expect of his behavior and offer him some reasonable, clear boundaries for this behavior? To do so is simply good dog "parenting." After all, your dog's behavior toward you is, in great part, a measuring stick of your behavior toward your dog.

Just loving the dog is not enough. Combining strong leadership with a clear job description and a good dose of team spirit is what it's about. Complicating the relationship with guilt is a senseless waste of time—a senseless waste of the dog's time, anyway. Dogs who are loved more do not necessarily feel more loved. Dogs who play an integral role in their own groups' effort do. Dogs who wait, day after day, for the sacred pack to return, with little else to do, are literally petri dishes for behavioral problems. Dogs who wait because it is a part of their job to do so are healthy dogs. If your dog spends a good deal of his time waiting, then waiting must be part of his job, not just empty space. And, the chances are, if your dog does not do what you want, it's because he really doesn't know what you want.

Dogs are not autonomous creatures. Leaving them to their own devices will only breed troubled behavior. The more time I spend helping people perfect their human-canine relationships, the clearer it becomes that the people part of the relationship needs some clarification. More and more people are spending valuable time and money making excuses for their dog's behavior instead of simply gaining an understanding of the way the relationship needs to be structured in order to thrive. Discrediting the theory that a dog's life needs to be structured within boundaries of leadership and discipline in order to justify "free love" is simply a gateway to all kinds of behavioral problems.

Not too long ago, during a training session with a woman and her extremely aggressive young dog, the woman adamantly stated that she loved her dog and that creating boundaries within their relationship would only place limits on this love. She found that she had a rather difficult time applying (even in theory) the basic principles of structure to their relationship. As she put it: "If I am not free to love this dog and this dog is not free to love me, then why have the dog at all?" She ultimately made the decision not to structure the dog's life, but instead to "talk him through" any behavioral issues that might arise. To the woman, I say, "Good luck," and to the dog, I say, "Happy hunting." Once the decision to live with a dog has been made, the very next decision should be to better understand how to live with a dog. So much information is available to us today and yet so many of us choose the road paved with emotional potholes, bypassing altogether the actual information highway.

I often watch my five-year-old daughter interacting with my own dogs. Her messages are so pure. She requires little in return for the Cheerios that she shares and even less for her endless affection. She spends countless hours on the floor indulging the dogs in play and sleeps on them like pillows when it is time to rest.

Seeing how these dogs revel in her affection makes me sometimes wish I knew less about animal behavior. If that were the case, then I, too, would be at liberty to give my affection away without a price—indulging them without a reason. But, because of my understanding of how the canine mind works, I know that my dogs perceive my child as a lesser-ranking pack member. They do not look to her for direction and security. They treat her as a subordinate and do not rely on her for safety but, instead, feel the need to keep her safe.

It is this dynamic that continually confirms my conviction that we must respect what needs to be respected. Dogs cannot and should not be required to stray from the psychological boundaries that keep them healthy and whole. The complex social structure of a group hierarchy that has sustained their species for thousands of years deserves to be respected and upheld. And if they are going to live with us, it is we who must sustain the hierarchy.

As we the people pick up our leashes and step into yet another century with our beloved dogs at our sides, let us be careful to tread softly. Dogs are necessarily codependent creatures who rely on their leaders to keep them strong. As their leaders, it is our responsibility to remember that—while we continue to search for better ways to coexist with our canines—we are not the same animal.

So, if you are currently contemplating quitting your job or, at the very least, working out of your garage because you can't stand to be apart from your dog, or if you're drawing straws about who's going to tell the dog that he's really a dog, just remember—if nothing else, your dog deserves the benefit of your understanding. Patience, instruction, and a viable job are the things our dogs need—okay, food and water, too.

The bottom line is that the time has clearly come for every card-carrying member of Dog Lovers Anonymous to admit that we have gone too far or, at least, that we might be going too fast. When the bill for your dog's therapist is almost double yours, and the dog walker is at your house more often than you are, your wallet isn't the only thing suffering—so is your dog.

As thankful as I am to have had the good fortune of having spent my own childhood with dogs, as well as raising my children in the company of dogs, I am even more grateful for the insight I have gained into how necessary it is to know *how* to live in the company of dogs. For it is the way in which we live with our dogs that makes the greatest difference in the quality of our relationships—and, ultimately, the quality of their lives.

Index